Praise for *Whistle* [barcode obscures text]

"Sharp and engrossing . . . A powerful i[obscured] our society continues to throw up in the [obscured] young women, and the ways that institutions s[obscured]ect and enable badly behaving men." —*The New York Times Book Review*

"This is not just a book for people interested in the culture of Silicon Valley. Like all the best books, it delivers the reader into a fully drawn world she may never have imagined. . . . At times it reads like a spy thriller, at others like a satire of what might happen when corporate overlords go unchecked. . . . The details around her experience at Uber are the sizzle; Fowler's own story is the steak. . . . That she became a whistleblower and a pioneer of a social movement almost seems inevitable once you get to know her. Uber should have seen her coming." —*San Francisco Chronicle*

"It's easy to focus on what happened to Fowler . . . but in her new memoir, Fowler makes a dedicated plea for you to focus, instead, on what she did about it. . . . [*Whistleblower*] does provide more eyebrow-raising details about just how hostile and chaotic Uber's workplace was. But Fowler is much more interested in unpacking how—and why—she responded by going public. . . . This memoir is a bit of a how-to book, too, with some take-home lessons for anyone discouraged by a hostile workplace." —*NPR.org*

"Gut-wrenching . . . One of several newly published memoirs—all of them written by women—that complicate that mythology [of whistleblowing] and engage in more diffusive acts of revelation. These works are not exposing discrete instances of corruption or corporate malfeasance. Instead, they are exposing corrupt cultures. . . . Fowler's story—her full story—is the indictment. That is what gives *Whistleblower* its power." —*The Atlantic*

"[An] earnest retelling of one woman's effort to go to school and do her job in environments that were actively hostile to her existence and well-being. . . . One can only imagine the alternate reality in which Fowler and her ilk were the ones hailed as geniuses and given all the money in this world to build a better one."

—*The Washington Post*

"[*Whistleblower*] broadens the view beyond Uber, offering a clear-eyed exploration of what workplace sexual discrimination looks like, why it's so toxic, and how it destroys ambitions, careers, and lives."

—*The Huffington Post*

"Despite the title of her book, Fowler defies one-word labels. She is a musician, a writer, a physicist, a philosopher. . . . She paints a picture of a ferociously independent and determined person."

—*The Guardian* (London)

"*Whistleblower* fills us in on how junior white-collar employees struggled to keep the culture [CEO Travis Kalanick] instilled from threatening their sanity, and how one of them was eventually able to tear it down."

—*Slate*

"American society did its very best to prevent [Fowler] from succeeding. Her life, and this book, represents her triumph over almost inconceivable odds."

—*Axios*

"[*Whistleblower*] shows the importance of having people who are of strong character, who are willing to stand up to some of the things they see going wrong at these companies and speak up about them."

—*Wired*

PENGUIN BOOKS

WHISTLEBLOWER

A contributing opinion writer and the former technology op-ed editor at *The New York Times*, Susan Fowler has been named a "Person of the Year" by *Time*, the *Financial Times*, and the Webby Awards, and has appeared on *Fortune*'s "40 Under 40" list, *Vanity Fair*'s New Establishment list, *Marie Claire*'s New Guard list, the Bloomberg 50, the Upstart 50, the Recode 100, and more. She is the author of a book on computer programming that has been implemented by companies across Silicon Valley and a forthcoming novel from William Morrow.

SUSAN FOWLER

WHISTLEBLOWER

MY UNLIKELY JOURNEY TO SILICON VALLEY
AND SPEAKING OUT AGAINST INJUSTICE

PENGUIN BOOKS

PENGUIN BOOKS
An imprint of Penguin Random House LLC
penguinrandomhouse.com

First published in the United States of America by Viking,
an imprint of Penguin Random House LLC, 2020
Published in Penguin Books 2021

"Reflecting on One Very, Very Strange Year at Uber" was originally published
on the author's blog on February 19, 2017. www.susanjfowler.com
/blog/2017/2/19/reflecting-on-one-very-strange-year-at-uber.

ISBN 9780525560142 (paperback)

THE LIBRARY OF CONGRESS HAS CATALOGED THE
HARDCOVER EDITION AS FOLLOWS:
Names: Fowler, Susan J., author.
Title: Whistleblower : my journey to Silicon Valley and
fight for justice at Uber / Susan Fowler.
Description: [New York] : Viking, [2020] |
Identifiers: LCCN 2019034425 (print) | LCCN 2019034426 (ebook) |
ISBN 9780525560128 (hardcover) | ISBN 9780525560135 (ebook)
Subjects: LCSH: Sexual harassment—California—Santa Clara Valley (Santa
Clara County) | Sexual harassment of women—California—Santa Clara
Valley (Santa Clara County) | Whistle blowing—California—Santa Clara
Valley (Santa Clara County) | Uber (Firm)—Corrupt practices.
Classification: LCC HD6060.5.U52 S36 2020 (print) |
LCC HD6060.5.U52 (ebook) | DDC 305.42092 [B]—dc23
LC record available at https://lccn.loc.gov/2019034425
LC ebook record available at https://lccn.loc.gov/2019034426

Printed in the United States of America
1 3 5 7 9 10 8 6 4 2

Designed by Amanda Dewey

Some names and identifying characteristics have been changed
to protect the privacy of the individuals involved.

To my daughter

*It is my hope that when you are old enough to read
this book, the world described within it is completely
unrecognizable to you; that you, and the women of
your generation, will live in a world where you
can chase your dreams without fear of harassment,
discrimination, and retaliation—a world where
the only thing you have to fear is whether
your dreams are big enough.*

WHISTLEBLOWER

PROLOGUE

"It's important that you don't share the details of this meeting—or that this meeting even happened—until after the investigation has concluded."

Sitting directly across from me, asking me to keep our meeting secret, was the former U.S. attorney general Eric Holder. His hands were clasped together, his elbows resting on the table, a plastic binder filled with notes open before him. To his left sat Tammy Albarrán, a partner at the corporate law firm Covington & Burling. She stopped combing through her own notes for a moment and held her pen in her hand, staring at me over the dark rectangular frames of her glasses, awaiting my answer.

"I understand," I said, nodding. Albarrán crisply put her pen back down to her notes.

Two months earlier, I had written and published a blog post about my experiences as a software engineer at the ride-sharing company Uber Technologies. In the blog post, which I had titled "Reflecting on One Very, Very Strange Year at Uber," I described being propositioned by my manager on my first official day on Uber's engineering team; the extent to which Uber's managers, executives, and HR department had ignored and covered up harassment and discrimination; and the retaliation I'd faced for reporting illegal conduct. It was a meticulously, cautiously, deliberately crafted portrait of the company, one that I had constructed with almost excruciating care, every sentence backed up by written documentation.

My story quickly caught the attention of the media and the public. Several hours after I'd shared a link to it on Twitter, it had been retweeted by reporters and celebrities and was a "developing story" covered by local, national, and international news outlets. Travis Kalanick, then the CEO of Uber, shared a link to my blog post on Twitter and said, "What's described here is abhorrent & against everything we believe in. Anyone who behaves this way or thinks this is OK will be fired." He then hired Eric Holder and Holder's firm, Covington & Burling, to run a thorough investigation into the company's culture. It was clear that Kalanick wanted to send a message: he was taking this seriously—so seriously that anyone involved in what had happened, anyone responsible for the story that was now being repeated by every major news outlet across the globe, would be fired.

Three days later, *The New York Times* published its own damning account of Uber's culture. The day after that, Waymo, a subsidiary of Google that was developing self-driving cars, sued Uber for patent infringement and trade secret theft. Less than a week later, a video leaked of Travis Kalanick berating an Uber driver. And that was only the beginning. By the time I found myself across the table from President Obama's attorney general, the public consensus was that something was very wrong with Uber, but nobody was quite sure of the extent of the problem or who should be held responsible for it. "Some people," Kalanick had shouted at the driver in the grainy dashcam video, "don't like to take responsibility for their own shit."

As the drama unfolded in the press, I waited. I didn't know what was going to happen, and everything—including my fate, the fate of my ex-coworkers, and the fate of Uber—seemed to be riding on the results of the Covington & Burling investigation. I'd been reluctant to meet with Eric Holder, afraid that I would mess everything up, that I would say the wrong things, that I would somehow jeopardize the investigation. But now that I was sitting across from him, there was so much I wanted to say, and I didn't know where to start. I didn't know how much I should tell him, how much I should leave out. I wondered if I should tell him about my coworker's suicide, about the private investigators who seemed to be following me everywhere, about the rumors Uber was spreading about me and my husband, about how I'd heard that Uber had been destroying documentation in order to conceal its mistreatment of employees.

As I sat there, my mind racing, I looked up at him.

"Start from the beginning," he said.

I wasn't supposed to be a software engineer. I wasn't supposed to be a writer, or a whistleblower, or even a college graduate, for that matter. If, ten years ago, you had told me that I would someday be all of those things—if you had shown me where life would take me, and the very public role I would end up playing in the world—I wouldn't have believed you.

I grew up in poverty in rural Arizona and was homeschooled until my early teens; after that, my mother had to return to the workforce and, unlike my younger siblings, I couldn't go to public school, so I was on my own. As a young teenager, I worked below-minimum-wage jobs during the day and tried to educate myself at night. I feared my life was heading in the same direction as that of many other teenagers living in the rural Southwest—toward drugs, unemployment, and trailer parks. But I refused to accept this as my fate, and resolved to fight for a better life. I worked very hard to educate myself, and managed to get into college.

The struggle to determine my own direction in life didn't end there. When I wanted to study physics at Arizona State University, but couldn't because I didn't have the necessary prerequisites, I transferred to the University of Pennsylvania. When I was also prevented from studying science and mathematics at Penn, I once again fought for the education I so desperately wanted and believed I deserved. After my dream of becoming a physicist was derailed by an incident with a male student in my lab, I had to choose an entirely new career, which led me to Silicon Valley. If you're reading this book, you probably know the story of what happened next: I was sexually harassed and bullied at Uber, and I fought until I had exhausted all options except one—to leave the company and go public with my story.

Over the years, I have often thought of a quotation from the philosopher Isaiah Berlin's "Two Concepts of Liberty": "I wish my life and decisions to depend on myself, not on external forces of whatever kind. I wish to be the instrument of my own, not of other men's, acts of will. I wish to be a subject, not an object; to be moved by reasons, by conscious purposes, which are my own."

This book is the story of my journey to become the subject, not the object, of my own life—to be the person who *made things happen* rather than the woman who *had things happen to her.*

Throughout this journey, I have often turned to the words and stories of others for courage and inspiration—Fred Rogers, Rainer Maria Rilke, Fyodor Dostoevsky, Hannah Szenes, and Anne Sexton; the philosophers Aristotle, Plato, Epictetus, Marcus Aurelius, Seneca, Immanuel Kant, and Martha Nussbaum. Thanks to their words, a lot of hard work, and great determination—along with the support of family and friends and, later, my husband, Chad—I made it through to the other side.

In sharing the story of my life, I want to offer the same courage and inspiration to others. I hope this book will help those who find themselves in situations like the ones I describe; that it will help them see the steps they can take and the challenges and choices they will face; that it will help them find greater autonomy in their lives and help them discover that they have the power to become the heroes and protagonists of their own stories. In its pages is the kind of story I wish someone had shared with me when I was younger: the story of a young woman who managed to take fate into her own hands and speak up against injustice, even though she was afraid to do so.

CHAPTER ONE

Even though I was born in Michigan, I have always considered Arizona my home. When I was six years old, my father drove our family from our rental home behind a Kmart parking lot in Traverse City, Michigan, to a little white ranch house in Congress, Arizona. The house was located on a working cattle ranch and had once been a bunkhouse where cowboys slept whenever they drove the cattle south across the Sonoran Desert. At the time, there were seven of us: me; my father, John; my mother, Cheryl; my three sisters, Elisabeth, Martha, and Sara; and my little brother, John. After my two youngest brothers, Peter and Paul, were born, we moved a few miles northeast to Yarnell, where my father worked as a preacher. Home to barely six hundred people, Yarnell was hidden away at the top of a large desert mountain range known as the Weaver Mountains; the only way to get there was to drive a winding and sometimes dangerous road up what locals called Yarnell Hill.

The area where I grew up was about as rural as you could get in the modern American West. Surrounded by cattle ranches on all sides, thirty minutes from the nearest real store, and almost an hour away from the closest hospital, these small towns were filled with people who had been left behind, along with the occasional person who was running away from something. Some of our neighbors were ranchers and some were tradespeople, but most of them lived on government assistance and spent their days sitting alone in their small mobile or modular homes in the local trailer parks.

Like our neighbors, we were very poor. One year, I overheard my mother telling my father that they'd made five thousand dollars that year—a sum that sounded like a lot at the time, but now only reminds me of the level of poverty I was raised in. Because the money my father received for preaching was barely enough to pay for our groceries, he always had to work a second job as a door-to-door salesman: first for Kirby, selling vacuums; then for MCI and AT&T, selling pay phones. When the cell phone came on the scene and pay phones became a thing of the past, he started selling life insurance. My father worked very hard, but no matter how hard he worked, he wasn't able to pull our family out of poverty. We got by, but just barely. The more well-to-do members of the church would drop boxes of food and clothing at our front door, and various friends and relatives often sent checks to help my parents pay their bills: twenty-five dollars here, a hundred there—it all added up.

Despite our poverty, I had a wonderful childhood. Our home was filled with love and happiness. My parents did their best to stay upbeat, even when we didn't have any food in the fridge, when our plumbing stopped working and we had to go to the bathroom outside, or when we didn't have hot water and my mother had to boil water for us to bathe in. Our neighbors and friends were just as poor as we were, and some of them had it so much worse that our family seemed well-off in comparison.

When we moved to Yarnell, we lived in the parsonage—a yellow three-bedroom, one-bathroom house owned by the church. My three sisters and I shared a room with two beds, the three boys shared a room with one bunk bed, and our parents took the smallest room for themselves. The house was old and in desperate need of work. There were times when we had no running water, no electricity, no working sewer. When the monsoon rains came in the late summer, the girls' bedroom would flood as the rain poured through the seams of the old fireplace in the middle of our room.

My siblings and I spent most of our time outside. The churchyard was a natural playground, strewn with big, tangled bushes, gigantic oak trees, and enormous granite boulders. We loved that yard, and we played in it day in and day out, building forts, digging ditches, being chased by wild animals, and re-creating scenes from the old movies we borrowed from the library. I'll never forget flying down the gravel driveway with my brothers and sisters, our heads tilted toward the sky as we pretended to be Eric Liddell from *Chariots of Fire*. Those were wild and wonderful years, filled with adventures rivaling those of my childhood hero Tom Sawyer. The Sonoran Desert was my Mississippi River, and I spent every free moment running through the dust. Whenever I was outside, I had complete freedom—freedom to explore, to create, to play— and it was a freedom that I never wanted to live without.

While my father went door-to-door, my siblings and I were home-schooled by our mother. Our parents homeschooled us because they wanted us to have a Christian-based education that was filled with more art and music and creativity than the local public schools offered. A resourceful and wonderful teacher, my mother studied homeschooling curricula carefully and made sure that we were learning the things we needed to know: reading, writing, math, history, science, music. Each weekday, all seven little Fowler children would sit around the kitchen table doing schoolwork, solving problems in workbooks or reading textbooks and novels from the library. When we were done with our schoolwork, we ran outside and played in the dirt and climbed in the trees until our mother walked out to the front porch and rang the bell for dinner.

Some of my fondest childhood memories are of learning things from my mother. I remember sitting on her lap in front of her old sewing machine, learning how to thread the bobbin; I remember watching carefully as her rough fingers, calloused from years of playing the guitar, guided the fabric of a dress through the machine like an experienced navigator sailing through smooth waters (the dress was for me; she made almost all of our clothes herself). I remember how she would sit at the electric piano in our living room, her sharp black bob bouncing up and down as she played the notes that I was supposed to be playing on my violin; I remember how she would turn around, a serious look on her face and a smile in her eyes, and encourage me to play the notes both in time and in tune. And I remember how, before we could afford to buy that electric piano, she made us a paper piano out of poster board and permanent marker, and how she taught me to play that paper piano by singing the notes of the paper keys whenever I touched them.

Every Sunday, we walked over to the church where my father preached, and our whole family played music for the congregation: my father singing at the pulpit, my mother with a guitar and mic, me at the piano, Elisabeth on the violin, John on the drums, Martha and Sara singing into a mic, Peter and Paul sitting in the front pews below.

My parents were fiercely Evangelical. The Holy Spirit was very real to them, as were spiritual warfare and speaking in tongues. Neither of them had grown up religious; they had both converted to Christianity in their twenties. My father was a man of intense faith, a faith that challenged him; he once told me, when I asked him if he really believed, that he asked himself that all of the time, and that he would never stop asking.

Throughout my young life, I struggled to make sense of it all. I was raised in a Christian household, the daughter of an Evangelical preacher, but I always felt caught between worlds. Even though my mother was Christian, her side of the family was Jewish and German, and my siblings and I always partly identified as Jewish. Our parents also identified us as such: at the same time my father was telling me that I needed to pray to Jesus, he was giving me Hebrew lessons and telling me that he wished he could send me to Hebrew school; at the same time my siblings and I were watching the miniseries *Jesus of Nazareth*, we were wrestling with the

horrors of the Holocaust; at the same time my father was smug-
gling Bibles into China, we were trying to evade a group of neo-
Nazis and white supremacists who lived in our small town. But the
two belief systems were in conflict, and the tension ate at me: Was
I Christian or was I Jewish? I often felt that I was simultaneously
both and neither. As I grew older and watched one of my sisters
fully embrace Judaism, I visited Christian congregations and Jewish synagogues but never felt like I belonged.

Because of their strong religious convictions, my parents never
quite fit into the world. For many of the other people we knew,
faith was something around the periphery of life, something that
was part of their life but wasn't their life's main purpose. For my
parents, however, it *was* life: their faith was their reason for being.
Growing up, I was very much aware of the fact that they were different from other people, that they were outsiders, and I couldn't
help but wonder whether I was a bit of an outsider, too.

While my mother did manage to connect with like-minded
people, my father never really found a place where he belonged.
He was one of those rare people who seem as though they were
meant for another world, and he was a man of strong principles,
who desperately wanted to know the meaning and purpose of life.
When he was in his twenties, he made up his mind that the answer
to all of his questions might have something to do with the Christian God—the God of Abraham, the God of the prophet Isaiah,
the God of the apostle Paul. Being a man of principle, my father
decided that if what the Bible said was true, that if the God of the
Bible was real, then the only rational thing to do was to devote his
life to understanding the Bible and growing closer to God.

He was a biblical scholar who was especially gifted with languages. Over the years, he had learned Hebrew, Ancient Greek, and Aramaic so that he could read the Bible; Russian and Mandarin so that he could preach during his missions trips to Russia and China; and German, French, and Spanish just because he loved the languages. He had an insatiable hunger for knowledge, both religious and secular. At night, long after dinner had been cleared away, he would sit at the kitchen table with his notebooks and books in front of him, his head down, a pen in his hand, studying and learning. On his way to and from sales calls, he listened to foreign language tapes, and he never left home without his "book bag," a little black messenger bag that held his notebooks, pens, books, and Pimsleur cassettes. More than anything, he wanted to be a writer; he wrote several books and sent them to Christian publishers, but none of them were ever published. He also dreamed of someday preaching at a large church, and of never having to sell vacuums, pay phones, or insurance ever again. I know in my heart that he must have hated every moment of his work as a salesman, but I never heard him complain. And he never stopped learning—or dreaming.

Like my father, I had big dreams.

When I was around ten years old, I noticed that, every Sunday, an architecture firm in Phoenix would print the floor plan of one of their newest houses in the local paper. Until then, it had never occurred to me that buildings were designed by people—that each building had been dictated by a floor plan and a set of blueprints. I started cutting out the floor plans and would stare at them until I'd memorized the layout of each house; I would lie down on the floor, close my eyes, and try to imagine what the house looked like. Most of the houses in the plans were small and practical, but some of them were large, beautiful, and extravagant, featuring exotic things like courtyards and enormous staircases and extra rooms that could be used for things like libraries and music rooms. The world of these houses seemed completely foreign to me; I had seen very few houses that weren't small, dilapidated buildings like the one we lived in. "What kind of people live in this place?" I would wonder. I imagined what those families were like, wondered how they spent their days.

When my mother realized what I was doing, she flipped through her homeschooling supply catalogs and bought me the most promising book on architecture she could find. Thanks to that book, I learned how to draw blueprints, how to calculate building costs, how to alter existing buildings, and so much more. My simple daydreams soon turned into full-fledged custom-designed homes.

Throughout my childhood, I dreamed of becoming many things: an architect, a doctor, a lawyer, president of the United States. But my most pressing, most secret dream—the one I never told anyone, for fear they would laugh at me and tell me I couldn't do it—was to be a writer.

When I was around three or four years old, I stopped taking naps and had difficulty sleeping. While my siblings would drift off to sleep, I would lie there, my little mind racing, unable to slow my thoughts. My mother was at her wit's end, but then one of her friends from church suggested that she teach me how to read. In her catalogs she found a book called *Alpha-Phonics*, and every night, we sat in bed together and read one page of the book, until, a few months later, I was able to read. I never did nap again, but I was able to sleep through the night if I read enough books during the day to occupy and quiet my mind.

I read every book I could get my hands on—every book I could find in my father's collection, in the local bookstores, and at the library. I read anything and everything, from books about how to build wooden sailing ships to *The Saddle Club* and *Nancy Drew*. Whenever I read a book, I felt like I was living a whole new life, that I was exploring possibilities and seeing the world in ways that would otherwise be inaccessible to me. For example, I loved horses and wanted a horse of my own so badly it made my heart ache, and I knew my family could never afford one, but whenever I read a book about a girl who owned a horse, I got to pretend that I was her, and during those precious hours I had a horse of my own.

I thought that being a writer must be the most wonderful, important job in the world. Writers gave people new experiences, new lives, and new worlds to live in; it all seemed magical, almost supernatural. So I wrote, all the time. I wrote a short series of historical fiction novels about a girl who lived during the Great Depression. I sent articles to *Reader's Digest*. I began a lifelong habit of journaling obsessively about my days and the events that transpired in my simple life. I even wrote to one of my favorite horse magazines to ask if I could write a monthly column (the magazine's editors never responded).

Even as I dreamed of becoming a writer and an architect, the dream that truly felt within my grasp was becoming a professional violinist. After all, I thought, there was nothing to prevent a poor girl from playing the violin, as long as she had a violin and worked hard enough at it. And so I played my violin every single day for most of my young life. I played for hours and hours, until my fingers were so sore I could hardly move them. Sometimes, I'd close my eyes and pretend that I was playing in the Paganini Competition, up against the best violinists in the world. Sometimes, I saw myself surrounded by an entire orchestra: I'd walk out onto the stage, the audience waiting, the other players holding their breath, the conductor watching me carefully; I'd nod at the conductor and then, after the orchestra began playing, I'd count the measures until I jumped in, bringing my bow down to the strings to play the opening of Tchaikovsky's Violin Concerto.

Looking back, I believe that all this dreaming and reading and playing was a means of escape from the realities of my life. Even with all of its fun and joy and possibility, life was very hard on our family. When I was a young child, I was naive about my lot in life: I thought that everyone lived in poverty. I believed that the conditions of my life were normal, and I was happy in my ignorance. But as I grew older, I met people who'd had very different lives, and the severity of my own circumstances dawned on me. I struggled to make sense of my own feelings about it and couldn't figure out how to explain it to others. It's hard to explain to someone who has never slept in a dilapidated, run-down house what that feels like. It's hard to explain to people who have never wondered whether they will be able to eat what it's like to go hungry because your family doesn't have enough money to buy food. It's hard to explain what it's like to not be taken to the doctor when you're sick because your family can't afford to pay the hospital bill. It's hard to explain what it's like to not be able to drive to the grocery store because your parents can't afford a gallon of gas. Yet these were the realities of my life, the lives of my siblings, and the lives of the other children in my neighborhood.

I started working when I was ten or eleven. I don't remember being asked to do so; we were just so desperately poor that it seemed like the obvious thing to do. My first job was at the Spider Pharm, a small business down the street run by a family of Czech scientists. They owned and bred thousands upon thousands of venomous spiders, which they "milked" for venom they would then sell to research labs, hospitals, and universities all over the world. Each day, after I finished my schoolwork, I would go to their house for a few hours to feed the spiders and take care of the various creatures that the spiders ate—from mice (for the tarantulas) to fruit flies (whose larvae the smaller spiders loved to eat).

It was difficult, messy work. I will never forget the musty, fleshy stench of the fruit fly larvae, which would squirm around in gigantic plastic garbage bins that were the size of a kitchen sink; I fed them and cleaned their bins, trying not to let too many of them fall on the floor as I poured the maggots from one garbage bin into another. Sometimes, if I was lucky, I would get to open the sacs filled with spider eggs and very, very carefully put each egg into a little plastic container with tweezers. Other times, I fed maggots to the black widows and brown recluses, carefully lifting the lids off the spiders' tiny cages and dumping a few wriggling maggots inside for them to eat. I was bitten several times, but never harmed, because I learned on my first day that the spiders' fangs couldn't reach through the thick skin of my fingertips; as long as I didn't let the spiders near anything but my fingertips, I would be all right.

While I worked at the Spider Pharm, I had a side job at another local business called Brand New Dead Things. The owner was a kind old man named Paul who spent his days wandering through the desert, collecting geodes and insects and dead rodents. He ran a store in Yarnell, a few blocks from our house, that was filled with all of the things he had discovered, polished, skinned, and put into shadow boxes. Paul taught me and Elisabeth how to carefully pin butterflies and moths and large insects and frame them so that they looked professional; the prettily mounted insects were then sold to tourists, schools, and museums. There was a locust infestation in Yavapai County during one of the years we worked there, and for a few dollars an hour Elisabeth and I sat in the back of Brand New Dead Things for hours at a stretch, pinning and preserving hundreds upon hundreds of six- to eight-inch-long locusts.

When I was in my early teens, our family's financial situation reached a dire point, and my mother had to get a job. She started working as a bank teller in the nearby town of Wickenburg, which meant she could no longer homeschool me and my brothers and sisters. She was bitterly disappointed that she had to return to work, because she loved teaching us and spending time with us, but she didn't have much of a choice, and neither did we. My little brothers and sisters were enrolled in the local public schools and began attending real classes for the first time in their lives, but

Elisabeth and I were unable to go to school. I don't know exactly why this happened. I have memories of being told about state tests that we had never taken, about the difficulty of enrolling us in anything above elementary school (which we were too old to attend), and that we would have to be okay educating ourselves through high school, because it appeared there was no other option. Without any other choices available to us, we were completely on our own.

At first, I wasn't sure how to homeschool myself, but I eventually fell into a routine: I would work during the days, then read and teach myself things at night. Elisabeth seemed to have an easier time keeping up with what we would have learned in school; she bought books on mathematics and biology and conducted chemistry experiments in the bedroom we shared with our younger sisters. I, on the other hand, was initially incapable of doing much more than staring at beginner-level algebra books and crying over the pages because none of it made any sense to me. I watched jealously as my little brothers and sisters made friends, took classes, brought home piles of homework, and participated in sports, dance, and other school activities. I daydreamed about being able to go to school, and built an elaborate fantasy in my head about having a locker in which to put my books and school supplies, having friends to play and gossip with, having homework to do at night, having sports teams to play on and extracurricular activities to do. School sounded like heaven to me.

I had a brief taste of that heaven when Elisabeth and I both received small scholarships from a local nonprofit music organization; the scholarships came from an anonymous donor in the community who intended the money to be used for music classes. At the time, I still had my heart set on becoming a professional violinist, and over the last few years, I had played in competitions, bluegrass festivals, orchestras, and small ensembles. I played whenever I could and wherever I could and to whoever would listen to me. At this point, I was pretty damn good, and so was my sister. When we were awarded the scholarships, we jumped at the opportunity and used the money to take lessons at a community college in Prescott, a city located forty-five minutes northeast of Yarnell. For an entire year, we played in the college orchestra, studied music theory, and took private violin lessons. On the days we didn't have classes, we worked as many hours as we could at our below-minimum-wage jobs; while the scholarships paid for the tuition, we still had to pay for all transportation costs, our clothing, some of our food, our books, our college fees, and our lodging—all things our parents couldn't afford. Sometimes, our parents couldn't drive up to Prescott and pick us up until the next day, and neither of us was old enough to drive. Whenever this happened, we slept in bunk beds at a Christian summer camp that was empty during the school year; there was no heat and sometimes there wasn't any running water, but it was all we could afford.

I felt hopeful, thinking that perhaps I had solved my education problem. Dreaming of getting associate degrees, Elisabeth and I signed up for classes in other subjects and were horrified when our scholarships were promptly rescinded. The scholarships had come with a handful of restrictions that didn't quite make sense to us at the time, and in our eagerness to continue going to school, we had unwittingly violated one of those restrictions: apparently, taking non-music courses (even ones that were required for a degree in music) was grounds for us to lose our scholarships. We found ourselves right back where we'd started.

Around the same time, I took my violin bow to a local luthier to be re-haired. When my mother and I returned to his house to pick it up, he handed me the bow in two pieces. He told my mother that the bow had snapped in half while he was working on it. "It happens with old bows sometimes," he said, like that was supposed to comfort me. He wasn't able to fix it, and neither was anyone else within a hundred-mile radius. The loss of my bow was catastrophic: it was my competition bow, and without it, I simply couldn't play. The only other bow I had was a cheap plastic thing we'd bought for around thirty-five dollars that made my violin sound awful. I couldn't afford a new bow, so I was completely out of luck. Devastated, I loosened the strings on my violin, tucked it into the back of my closet, and didn't pick it up again for several years.

Having lost both my scholarship and my ability to play the violin, I spiraled into a dark depression. The thought of spending the rest of my teenage years working below-minimum-wage jobs and studying all alone was more than I could bear. Without my violin, I had lost my dream, my hope for the future, and the only path I knew to escaping my childhood poverty. I felt unmoored, lost at sea, like there was no reason for me to get up in the morning, no reason for me to keep going. I felt that I was stuck in some sort of purgatory: I didn't want to die, yet I didn't want to live the life I felt confined to. I didn't know what else I could do except keep living and hope that somewhere along the way I would find a better life.

The rest of my mid-teenage years were more of the same. I worked during the day—for a little while teaching violin to local elementary-school children, then as a stablehand, then as a nanny, and eventually in retail—and read books at night. I pretended that the authors of the books I read were my teachers, that the chapters of textbooks I read were the transcripts of lectures I was attending, and that when I read Plato's dialogues, I was sitting on the sidelines, eavesdropping on the conversations of Socrates. It was the loneliest time of my life.

Because I worked during the day, studied all night long, and didn't go to school, I didn't have many opportunities to meet people my own age. In an effort to protect me from drugs, sex, and other corrupting influences, my parents had strict rules about which friends I was and was not allowed to have: no female friends who did not go to church, no male friends whatsoever, and certainly no boyfriends. I got around the "no boyfriends" rule by dating girls whose families went to church, but we had to keep our relationships secret; being young women attracted to other young women (or, in my case, attracted to both young men and young women) was widely condemned in our community and by our families. Platonic friends were almost impossible to come by; whenever I did happen to meet people my own age, they rarely had any interest in being my friends, perhaps because I had become the stereotypical socially awkward, un-socialized homeschooled kid.

I feared that the rest of my life would be more of the same lonely, endless grind. I truly believed that it was over for me, that it was too late. I saw what my siblings were learning, I saw what other teenagers were learning, and I was painfully aware that I knew none of it. I had never taken a real test, I knew nothing about math beyond multiplication and division, I knew practically nothing about science. No matter how many books I read, I didn't believe there was any way I could ever catch up.

All I wanted was to be a normal kid, to go to school, to know things and to learn things, to have the chance to be smart, to have the same opportunities that were available to other kids my age. I'd tried to get into school after my brief community college experience, but for some of the same reasons I hadn't been able to enroll in public school in the first place, the high schools wouldn't take me. I couldn't afford to take classes at the local community colleges and universities, and I was too young to qualify for financial aid. My pain only became more unbearable when Elisabeth was admitted (with financial aid) to a community college in Phoenix; when I applied to the same school, they rejected me.

I knew where my life was headed. It was obvious. After all, what paths in life were open to a poor, white-trash woman in a rural town without any formal education? I looked around at the other young women in my town. They, too, had grown up in poverty. They, too, had no opportunity to escape, no hope, no future. Even the ones who'd managed to graduate from high school never made it out of poverty: many of them were addicted to drugs, living with their parents, living in trailer parks, living on food stamps and welfare because they couldn't find anything but part-time, minimum-wage jobs. That—or worse—was my future, and it hurt. God, it hurt. I cried myself to sleep most nights.

Then, one day, I snapped.

I remember the exact moment it happened. I was around fifteen or sixteen years old, sitting in my father's small office, surrounded by his books and bookcases, searching through the piles of books and trying to find one I hadn't yet read. It was early in the morning, my siblings were all at school, and I had a few hours to myself before I had to leave for my job as a nanny. As I sat there among the books that I had been reading for the last few years, thinking about the stories that they told of great people and the great things they had done, it suddenly occurred to me: these were stories about people who had *done things* in their lives, not had things *done to them*, who had *made things happen* in their lives, not had things *happen to them*.

In that moment, I thought of Epictetus, a Greek slave who became one of the greatest ancient philosophers, who taught that anyone could have a meaningful and fulfilling life if they focused their energy on changing only the things that were in their power to change and finding peace with (or ignoring) the things in their life that they had no power over. I thought of Plato, whose dialogues had taught me that living a good life was accessible to anyone who lived a life dedicated to the search for knowledge and pursuit of virtue. And, in that moment, I realized that I needed to be—in the words of Isaiah Berlin—the subject, not the object, of my own life.

It was as if someone had flipped a switch in my brain, as if something in my subconscious finally recognized that my survival was contingent on fighting for a better life, and every part of me was ready to win that fight. I stood up and told myself that I would find a way. I would find a way to have a better life. I would find a way out of poverty. I would find a way to learn. I would find a way to go to college. I would find a way *out*. Nobody was going to help me, so I needed to pull my life together all by myself.

My plan was simple: I would carefully teach myself the exact things I needed to know in order to persuade a college to admit me. I would learn only the topics that I could approach without the help of a teacher, hope that they would be enough to get me in the door, and give up on the rest. Advanced math, science, and technology went out the window; I had tried to learn them on my own and failed miserably, and there was no point in spinning my wheels. I focused on foreign languages, history, literature, and philosophy. I called high schools, community colleges, and universities all over the country, explained my situation, and asked them what topics they taught their students, what textbooks they used, and what I needed to teach myself in order to get into college.

I looked into the admissions requirements of the top colleges and tried to fit myself into them as best I could. I needed a high school transcript, so I took the list of required courses that were supposed to be on every high school transcript and taught myself the ones that I could figure out on my own. I typed up my own transcript, wrote "Susan Fowler Home School" at the top of each page, and listed every single "class" I had taught myself and every book and textbook that I had read. For several years, every night after I came home from my various jobs, I would work on the homework problems in the high school textbooks I found on sale at the local used bookstores, keeping a record of every single homework problem so I could send them to the colleges. I needed a personal essay, so I wrote and rewrote my personal essay over and over and over again, trying to explain why I wanted to learn and go to college. I needed to take the ACT, so one day I showed up at a high school in Gilbert, Arizona, surrounded by high school students who had been practicing and preparing for this test for years, and took the first standardized test of my life. Finally, I needed recommendation letters from teachers, so I found professors who worked at local colleges and asked them to mentor me and help me, to teach me about their areas of expertise, then asked them for recommendation letters.

While I was doing everything I could to get into college, my parents were also working hard to make their lives better. They both loved teaching, so they had decided to pursue degrees in education; just like me, they were working during the day and studying late into the night. The transition was a painful one for my father: he walked away from his job at the church and never preached in front of a formal congregation again. Thanks to our busy schedules, I rarely saw my parents except on the weekends, when our family went to church together in Phoenix. On one of these weekend trips, my mother found a luthier in Tempe, Arizona, who wanted to take a crack at repairing my bow and offered to do it for no more than the cost of the parts. It was a challenging repair, one that everyone else had told us was impossible, but he approached it like a surgeon, delicately gluing the cracked bow together and strengthening it by adding small pieces of wood along the sides and sanding them down so that you couldn't even tell that it had once been broken. When we went to pick it up, I brought my violin with me and had to tune it in the shop because I hadn't played it in so long. Even though I was dreadfully out of practice, when I put the bow to the strings and heard my beautiful violin sing, I felt as if no time had passed. I felt whole again.

To my complete surprise, I scored very well on the ACT. So well, in fact, that I landed myself the largest merit-based scholarship offered by the biggest university in the state: Arizona State University.

CHAPTER TWO

My plan had worked. I was eighteen years old, enrolled as a fresh-man at Arizona State University, with a full scholarship to my name and the opportunity to learn anything and everything I'd ever dreamed of.

Before my first official semester began, I spent hours and hours sitting in front of my computer, scrolling through the extensive course listings and making lists of all the classes I dreamed of taking. I declared majors in philosophy and music, with a concentration in violin performance. Music, because it was in my blood; I felt that I was called to be a violinist. Philosophy, because I believed it held desperately needed answers to the questions that troubled me so deeply. Like my father, I'd never felt like I belonged in the world, and I thought that if I understood life or the nature of the universe a little better, then perhaps my place in the world would become evident to me. I wanted to know how I should live, what it meant to live a "good" life. I believed then, just as I believe now, that studying philosophy would help me discover those answers.

In late spring, I decided I couldn't wait any longer. Overwhelmed with excitement, I signed up for several summer classes. I moved into a small old house in Tempe, right next to ASU's main campus, with some musicians I'd met the previous year, and prepared to start my classes.

Shortly before the summer term began, I stopped at a tattoo parlor near campus and had my favorite lines from Ovid's *Amores* tattooed on my left arm: *Nitimur in vetitum semper, cupimusque negata*. Striving after the forbidden—that is what I had done, for all of these years, and I wanted a permanent reminder, one that I would see in the mirror every single morning. What had been denied me, what had been "forbidden," was a formal education and personal autonomy, and now that I finally had my chance to learn and determine my future for myself, I wasn't going to squander it.

As soon as classes began, I threw myself into my schoolwork and my new life. Every day, I packed up my violin and my textbooks, walked down the street, and rode the free shuttle bus to campus. I worked hard in my classes, started making friends, and played the violin every day. Ever since my bow had been repaired, I'd been taking lessons from a teacher the luthier in Tempe had recommended—an ASU professor emeritus named Frank Spinosa, who took on only a few new students each year. Every day, I practiced Tchaikovsky's Violin Concerto—the solo piece I had chosen for the orchestra auditions that fall—and the first violin part of a Shostakovich—the orchestral piece that I had to play for the audition—until my fingers ached and my shoulders were stiff. For the first time in my young life, I felt like I was almost "normal": I was in school, I had friends, and I only had to work part-time. My tuition was mostly covered by my scholarship, so I only needed to scrape up enough money to pay for my housing and food. To make ends meet, I worked at a Christian bookstore in Scottsdale. I lived as cheaply as I could, which wasn't all that hard; it was really the only way I knew how to live.

It was a glorious summer. But as excited as I was to begin my undergraduate education, the victory was bittersweet. ASU hadn't been my first choice; several other colleges had offered me scholarships, but my father was diagnosed with brain cancer around the time when I was supposed to decide which school I wanted to attend. After his diagnosis, the decision was no longer a matter of comparing philosophy departments and music programs; the only thing that mattered was being close to my father. His oncologist told our family that he would live at least until Christmas, and I wanted to have as much time as I could with him before he died.

Just after he was diagnosed, when he was still well enough to leave the house, we visited the ASU campus together for new student orientation. He was so proud of me; I could see it in his eyes and in the grin he kept trying to hide while we walked around the campus, learning about the classes and extracurricular activities that would now be available to me. As we drove home later that day, he told me some of the things he'd loved most about his college education: the foreign-language classes he'd taken, the friends he'd made, the adventures he'd had, the things he'd learned about himself. Excited, I showed him the Greek and Latin classes I'd signed up for. As I enthusiastically asked him whether I should take a history course or an ancient mythology course to satisfy a requirement, I caught a glimpse of his face: he was smiling one of the biggest smiles I'd ever seen.

My father's health was failing quickly. By the middle of the summer, when I went home to see him, he didn't seem to recognize or remember me. He was in and out of the hospital, and that was where I preferred to visit him. Seeing him at home was too painful: he was still surrounded by his books and notebooks and favorite World War II movies, but he didn't read or talk; he didn't do anything except sit on the couch and stare at the wall. It was less jarring, it all felt less real somehow, to see him in the hospital, where he was surrounded by other people suffering from terminal illness, and didn't seem so terribly out of place.

One day, right before my orchestra audition, I'd been practicing my violin for hours and hours, but my nerves wouldn't calm down. This audition was *the big one.* It was the one that would determine whether I would place into the university orchestra. It was the one that would determine whether I would be a music major with a concentration in violin performance. It was the one that would determine whether I would follow my dream of becoming a professional violinist. I couldn't stop counting down the hours before I'd have to stand in front of a panel of judges and hope that they picked the measures of the Shostakovich that I could play well, hope that I didn't mess up the second page of the Tchaikovsky, hope that my hands didn't shake too much when I played my scales, hope to God I could remember how to play whatever scale they asked me to play. I knew that talking to my father would help me gather my courage, so I hopped on a bus and went to see him.

A few days earlier, he'd been moved into a hospice in Mesa, only a thirty-minute bus ride from the university. I arrived at the hospice early in the evening, and as my bus pulled up to the stop, I saw my mother's old beige minivan pull into the parking lot. As soon as I saw the look on her face, I knew why she and my brothers and sisters were there. "I tried to call you," she said, as she wrapped her arms around me. Together, we walked back to his room. When I saw him, I felt my heart stop. He looked so old and so frail. He didn't understand anything I said to him, and there was part of me that was glad for it, because I didn't know what to say. He passed away early the next morning, and I held his hand as he left this world behind and entered bravely into the next.

I don't remember much about the next few days. I remember that it rained the night after he died. I remember that my friend Chelsea wrapped her arms around me as I cried, and that she told me it was raining because the earth itself was grieving the passing of my father. I remember stumbling into the music department the morning of my audition, feeling disconnected from my body as I sat on the floor backstage and waited for someone to call my name. I remember walking out onto the brightly lit stage and staring out at the dark rows of empty seats—rows that seemed to stretch as high as I could see, running straight up, on and on and up and up into the darkness until they reached the very ends of the universe. I remember standing there, floating above my body, the panel of judges to my right, the rows of seats before me, and thinking that if I just walked off the edge of the stage and followed the rows of seats all the way up to the heavens, maybe someone would be there waiting for me. I remember the judges asking me multiple times to play a scale, but I couldn't understand what they were saying, and so I played A minor because it was the only scale I could remember how to play. I remember that they looked at one another and asked me to play my piece, and that I managed to start the Tchaikovsky, but I couldn't get very far past the beginning; I wanted to play those first measures of the melody again and again and again, louder and louder until the sound was so great and angry and sorrowful that it filled all those empty rows.

They never asked me to play the Shostakovich.

I didn't make the orchestra. Instead, I was placed in one of the lower community ensembles. Worse still, it appeared that I hadn't even been assigned to a violin instructor. The failed audition had effectively killed my chances of being a music major who specialized in violin performance, and, with that, my chances of becoming a professional violinist.

Everything I knew and loved about my life had been turned upside down. Our family, as I had always known it, would never be the same. My father was no longer alive. I would never again see him sitting at the kitchen table, conjugating his Greek verbs or reading one of his favorite books by Teddy Roosevelt. I couldn't bear knowing that he had gone through life without achieving any of his dreams, and I feared that I would suffer the same fate. My violin career—a dream that had begun the first time I picked up a violin when I was a little girl—was over. And it had ended not with a bang but with an endless, aching silence.

When the fall semester began, I struggled through the first weeks of classes, but I was a shell of my former self. I couldn't sleep, I couldn't eat, I couldn't think, I couldn't even cry; one of my sisters later told me that everyone thought I was drunk all of the time because I walked around in such a stupor. Eventually, I broke down. I withdrew from courses for the semester and checked myself into a mental health facility. There, sequestered from the world for a few days, I finally allowed myself to grieve. I grieved not only the passing of my father and the end of my lifelong dream, but also the loss of my childhood.

In the weeks that followed, I wrestled with the losses I had experienced and wondered where life was going to take me. I felt terrible guilt and sadness for failing my audition, and had to live with the knowledge that I was responsible for the end of my own dream. I tried to find hope in the situation, and wondered if I was meant for something else, if maybe the universe had other plans for me that were somehow more important or more fitting than becoming a violinist. Telling myself that there was some purpose or meaning behind the loss made me feel better; if there was something more, if there was something else in store for me, then there was a chance I could survive the hurt and learn to find peace with the loss. But what if I was wrong? What if the universe didn't have any plans for me? The idea that the abrupt end of my lifelong dream was just a random accident—that there might not be any meaning or purpose behind it—was terrible to contemplate.

I tried so hard not to think about it, tried not to let my mind dwell on his passing, but my father's death weighed heavily on me. I missed him terribly, and I couldn't admit to myself that he was really gone. Every few weeks, I'd have the same dream: that he hadn't died, he'd just gone away on one of his sales calls, or he'd been away on one of his missions trips to Russia or China. I wonder now if I was grieving over my failed violin audition as a distraction from the one loss I didn't want to wrestle with.

I wanted so badly to ask my father for help, the way I used to in my early teenage years. After my mother had cleared dinner away, he'd be sitting at the kitchen table in his favorite ugly old wooden chair that nobody else liked, his books and notebooks strewn across the table in front of him. "Hey, Dad," I'd say, "want to go for a walk?" He'd smile and say, "Sure, Susan, why not." He'd know, as he always did, that I wanted to talk to him about something big—something I didn't understand, something that I felt was terribly important. We'd walk around the neighborhood until we figured something out. He rarely had the answers to whatever odd questions were on my mind, but, in a somewhat Socratic way, he would ask me what I was thinking, then ask me to clarify, then ask me what I was thinking again, until I'd thought and talked about it enough that it started to make sense to me. After he died, I wished more than anything that we could take one of those walks again.

When the fog of grief and depression finally began to lift, I started to revisit some of the thinkers who had changed my life over the years. I wanted to know, more urgently than ever before, what it meant to be a human being, to have dreams and goals, to live a good and meaningful life. And, as I read the works of the great philosophers, poets, and novelists, I determined that if I spent my time on earth trying to answer the big questions, I would live a full, happy, and satisfying life. I didn't know whether the answers lay in philosophy, literature, music, science, art, mathematics, or some combination of these, but I decided that I would use my college education to figure it out. I would, as my favorite poet, Rainer Maria Rilke, wrote, "live the questions," in the hope that someday I might, "gradually, without noticing it, live along some distant day into the answer."

I was determined to get back to school and make a fresh start, but first I had to survive the next few months. Because I'd withdrawn from classes, I didn't have anywhere to live; even though I'd paid for my dorm room, I wasn't able to live there, because nonstudents weren't allowed to live on campus. I'd given the university all the rent and food money I'd saved for the year, and now I was completely broke—and homeless. I tried to get government assistance but didn't qualify because of the scholarship money I'd received earlier in the year, even though it had gone to paying for my tuition. I slept in my car for a few weeks, stayed with my mother for several days, and did a bit of couch surfing, eventually finding a couch in a friend's living room that she was willing to rent out to me for a hundred dollars a month—the most I could afford. I was able to find a few hours of work each week, but it barely covered my expenses. I sold everything I could just to survive—my laptop, extra musical instruments, clothes, books—and I skipped most meals because I couldn't afford to eat.

During those months, my weight dropped down to between eighty and ninety pounds. But I refused to give in to despair: I was determined to return to school, continue my education, and figure out how to live a meaningful life. Day after day, I told myself that my circumstances were only temporary, that I'd just had a rough streak, that I was going to start classes the next semester and be an amazing student and find my new path in life.

Excited and a bit terrified, I carefully picked my spring classes and counted down the days until school started.

That first day back at school was one of the happiest days of my life.

This time around, I had only one major: philosophy. Over the next year and a half, I packed my course schedule with philosophy classes. I loved every moment, every class, every paper, every homework problem, every test, and all of my wonderful professors. I was thriving, and I had the grades to prove it: I made the dean's list each semester. All the philosophy books I'd read and studied over the past several years had given me a solid foundation, and soon I was taking advanced graduate courses in philosophy alongside the requirements for my major. Sitting in those classes, learning about epistemology and ethics and logic, I began to piece together in my mind a picture of the world that finally made sense to me. I'd gone through my whole life feeling that I didn't understand the way the world worked, why people acted the way they did, or what life was supposed to be about, but in those classes, I finally began to find some answers.

I made wonderful friends in the philosophy department—the kinds of friends I'd always dreamed of having, with whom I could discuss the things I cared about. For the first time in my life, I was no longer an outsider: I'd met a group of people who, just like me, were interested in discovering the best ways to live, who wanted to know how the world worked. Within this group, I wasn't the weirdo, the social outcast, the awkward homeschooled kid; I was just *me*.

My closest friend was Shalon. We were almost twins, with our black hair and our nearly identical tattoos. On the night we met, I was standing in line for a show in downtown Phoenix, when she walked out of the venue. A mutual friend introduced us, and we stood there together, chain-smoking cigarettes and talking about how much we loved film, art, history, philosophy, and literature. I don't remember anything else about that night—not the band, not the people I came to the show with, not even the name of the venue—only that I met my best friend. It seemed at the time, as it still does now, that we were meant to meet each other.

During my sophomore year, I had to take an introductory science course to fulfill the general science requirement, so I signed up for astronomy. Until then, I knew practically nothing about science except what I'd managed to pick up in casual conversation and from my homeschooling textbooks. I was blown away by the class— I couldn't believe that human beings knew so much about the universe, that we'd discovered so much about its nature. We knew about stars and galaxies; we knew when and how the universe began and where it ended. We'd sent men to the moon, put a space station into Earth's orbit, built telescopes on land and in the sky that could reliably tell us what was happening in the universe around us today and what had happened in the rest of the universe millions and billions of years in the past. The most exciting thing of all was that there was still so much left to be discovered.

Determined to learn more, I went to the professor's office hours one afternoon and told him that I was in love with the things we were learning. I asked him what I needed to study in order to know everything that scientists knew about the universe, and I truly meant *everything*. He encouraged me to study physics, and told me about the mathematics and physics courses I would need to take for a physics major. Before I left, he suggested I read Richard Feynman's *Lectures on Physics*.

I didn't understand everything in Feynman's *Lectures*, but I understood enough that I knew I needed to study physics. Eager and excited, I tried to sign up for physics courses the following semester, but wasn't able to, because I didn't have any of the prerequisites. I went to the registrar and asked if I could register for math and physics courses and double major in philosophy and physics. Again I was met with a very firm but gentle "no," because, they explained, I didn't have the necessary math and science prerequisites from high school. No, because I would have to take a few years of remedial high school mathematics before I even came close to meeting the prerequisites for ASU's introductory physics and math courses. No, no, no, no. I prodded and pushed and searched for every loophole; I begged and presented emotional appeals, but it was no use.

My heart was set on studying physics; there was no way around it—I had to understand the nature of the universe—and I knew that I couldn't stay at ASU. I'd have to find another way. Transferring to another state school, such as the University of Arizona, wasn't an option, because every state school seemed to have the same requirements. I began to form a hypothesis, however, that if I were admitted to a top-tier school, like one of the Ivy League universities, they would let me study physics. After all, I reasoned, if they believed I was smart and qualified enough to be admitted, surely they would also believe that I was smart and qualified enough to take their introductory math and physics courses. I crossed my fingers and applied to every top-ranked school in the country that admitted transfer students. When all the acceptance letters (and several rejections) came in, I decided to start my junior year at the school that had the highest-ranked physics department: the University of Pennsylvania.

CHAPTER THREE

I've often wondered what might have happened if I'd stayed at Arizona State University, where I felt I belonged, where I had professors who believed in me, where I had friends like Shalon. Looking back, I sometimes wonder if I should have pushed harder at ASU, if maybe I should have spent a few extra semesters taking the math and physics prerequisites at local community colleges, if maybe I could have found some magical way to persuade the school to let me study math and physics. ASU was a remarkable, generous school, one that made peculiar students like myself feel at home. Unfortunately, Penn turned out to be a very different place.

At Penn, I was an outsider. Among my peers, many of whom had attended prestigious private schools, played sports like rugby and tennis, and came from wealthy families, I stuck out like a sore thumb. For new student orientation, the university rented out the entire Philadelphia Museum of Art, and all of the new students, both freshmen and transfers, had the run of the place for an entire night. While many of the students danced in the entrance and on the stairs, I walked through the rest of the empty museum, enjoying the exhibits on my own—partly because I loved the art and partly because the ostentation made me feel uncomfortable. When I went to one of the school cafeterias for the first time, I had to put some of the food back because it was terribly expensive and I couldn't afford to pay for it. As I stood at the register, trying to figure out what I should get rid of, the girl standing behind me tapped me on the shoulder. "Just put it on your student ID card," she said with a smile. "That way your parents will pay for it." I didn't know how to begin to tell her that my widowed mother, who was trying to keep my five younger siblings alive on her meager teacher's salary, and whose house the bank was trying to foreclose on, was definitely not going to be paying for my food. I would often call Shalon and fill her in on details of my new Ivy League life; she, too, had grown up in poverty and had made her way in the world all on her own; we were both astounded by the luxury and wealth that existed at Penn.

Even though I would've liked to fit in, and tried very hard to, I didn't mind being an outcast. I had big dreams, and I was certain that studying at Penn would help me achieve them. At convocation, I sat in the front row, wide-eyed and smiling in a big blue "PENN" sweatshirt, while the university president, Amy Gutmann, stood on the stage and told us that Penn would support all of our intellectual pursuits. I filled my schedule with several upper-level and graduate-level philosophy courses and was admitted to the sub-matriculation program, which would allow me to receive a master's degree in philosophy alongside my bachelor's degree. And, to my great joy, I also enrolled in my very first undergraduate math and physics courses.

The lowest-level math and physics courses offered at Penn were far beyond what I was capable of succeeding in. I was woefully behind my classmates: they had all taken AP calculus and AP physics in high school, while my math education had ended with long division. But I had known this would be my situation from the start, and I was determined to make it work. My life that first semester closely resembled my life before ASU, when I worked all day and studied late into the night: I went to classes all day, then walked home to an off-campus apartment I was renting, where I studied until I passed out from exhaustion. I had many years of catching up to do, so, in order to do the homework for my Penn courses, I studied various high school math and physics books, trying to bring myself up to speed.

By the end of the semester, I was so proud of myself. I'd aced my philosophy courses, and I'd gone from failing every single math and physics assignment and test to passing them. In the span of three months, I'd taken myself from the mathematics education level of a sixth grader to that of a somewhat competent (though in serious need of improvement) Ivy League student. I remember doing a lot of happy crying around that time. I felt like my life was a fairy tale: I'd turned myself from an uneducated, poor, forgotten kid into an Ivy League student who understood antiderivatives and Newton's Laws, and I'd done it all on my own.

Penn, unfortunately, did not see it the same way. When I went to register for the next semester's classes, I discovered that I'd been blocked from registering for any math or physics courses. Confused, I met with an academic advisor.

"We want to set you up for success," he told me, "and not for failure. Right now, you're failing."

I understood where he was coming from, but I thought that perhaps if I laid out the full picture, he might help me. I explained how I'd educated myself through high school, how I hadn't taken any of the prerequisites and had been studying high school algebra, precalculus, and trigonometry textbooks the entire semester to bring myself up to speed. I explained that, from my point of view, I'd succeeded this semester: I'd gone from knowing practically nothing and failing my assignments to passing my courses and really understanding the things I was learning in class.

He pushed back, saying that what I considered success was considered a serious failure at Penn, and that Penn didn't really like failures; I should be grateful, he said, that I could ace my philosophy classes, and I should stick with philosophy if I wanted to have any hope of graduating.

Heartbroken and frustrated, I tried to enlist the help of professors and classmates. I petitioned and begged and followed every bureaucratic protocol and process to the letter, and had no luck. But I wasn't ready to give up.

As I reflected on what to do, I thought of a story my mother had just told me: Not long before my father passed away, my parents bought a home. While I was preparing for college and trying to turn my life around, they'd been working to change their fortunes, too, enrolling in night classes at a local college and working toward their teacher certifications. They soon found teaching jobs at a public school in a small town just south of Phoenix, and our family's financial situation improved overnight.

They bought the house just after the housing bubble burst; it was one of those newer homes that had been built in response to increased lending, a house built to sell to someone who was borrowing far more than they could ever repay. After my father passed away, my mother began talking to her bank about refinancing her mortgage, hoping they would allow her to lower her monthly payments so she could keep more of her small salary. The bank agreed, and told her not to pay her mortgage during the refinancing process, so she set aside the money for those payments and awaited further news from the bank. Several months later, the bank informed her they would be foreclosing on the house. "You haven't paid your mortgage for several months now," they said. When she fought back, reminding them that they had told her not to pay her mortgage during those months, they said it didn't matter. They wanted to foreclose on the house, and they were going to do it now.

My mother was a widow with five children still at home, and she wasn't willing to lose the house that she had bought with my father—not without putting up a fight. She contacted bank executives, local news stations, and state representatives, but nobody came to her aid. She was almost ready to give up when she decided to try one last thing. "It's kind of crazy," she told me, "but I sent a letter to President Obama and asked him to help me. Someone from his administration contacted me, and together we found a way to save the house." My mother had saved her home by going to the very top. If I was going to save my education, I would have to do the same.

Inspired by my mother's bravery and persistence, I summoned up all of my courage and walked into the office of the university president, Amy Gutmann.

"I need to speak with President Gutmann," I said to her secretary. "In her speech at convocation, she promised that Penn would support our intellectual pursuits and help us achieve our dreams. I need her to make good on that promise."

I noticed President Gutmann standing by the doorway to her office. She was looking right at me.

"Could I go speak to her?" I asked. "It'll only take a moment."

"No," the secretary said. She grabbed a piece of paper from her desk and scribbled down an email address. "Here," she said, handing it to me. "Send her an email."

"Thank you so much," I said, tucking it into my backpack. "I will. Thank you!" When I looked back at the door to President Gutmann's office, it was closed.

Later that night, I sat down at my computer. I'd written plenty of impassioned emails asking people to help me in the past, but this was the first time I'd be emailing someone as powerful as the president of the University of Pennsylvania. There was a lot at stake, and she was my last hope. As I tried to figure out how to explain my situation to her, I felt myself growing even more frustrated. For as long as I could remember, all I had wanted was a formal education, the opportunity to learn and study the things I was passionate about. Here I was, at one of the best universities in the world, and I was still being held back. It wasn't right, and I wasn't going to settle for it.

"Dear President Gutmann," I began. "My name is Susan Fowler." I reminded her of her words at convocation and explained how they'd inspired me, then described the exasperating circumstances I was facing and asked for an in-person meeting. "I feel like my undergraduate education is failing me," I wrote.

Much to my surprise, she replied a few hours later, promising to fix things. I never did meet with her in person, but she spoke with the dean of the College of Arts & Sciences and the dean of college advising, and I was finally allowed to register for my physics and math courses. I'd taken a big bet on myself, and I'd persuaded the university to do the same.

During my second semester at Penn, I began to want more than classes and homework could teach me. If I was really going to understand the universe—and someday get a PhD in physics and become a real physicist—I would have to discover things myself, not merely learn about the things that other people had discovered. I considered the possible areas of research within the discipline—astrophysics, condensed matter physics, particle physics, cosmology, medical physics, and more—and all their different permutations.

Astrophysics, the study of the stars and galaxies and other celestial objects, was endlessly fascinating, but it didn't seem fundamental enough. Neither did cosmology, the study of the origin of the universe, nor condensed matter, the study of the properties of matter. As with philosophy, my ultimate aim in studying physics was to understand the universe around me and my place in it. For that reason, the branch of physics that most excited me was particle physics: the study of the elementary particles—the very building blocks of nature—and how they interact with one another. There were two branches of particle physics: theoretical, which was about developing and studying theories about fundamental particles (like electrons, photons, and quarks), and experimental, which was about testing those theories. Theoretical particle physics would have been the ideal thing for me to study, but I didn't have the mathematical track record needed to get my foot in the door, so I settled on experimental particle physics.

One of my new friends, Pavel, who was also studying physics and philosophy, had worked with the experimental particle physics group a few semesters earlier. With his encouragement, I applied for a research assistant position in the group. I'll never forget the moment I walked into the basement of the David Rittenhouse Laboratory for my interview. The hallways were lined with gigantic posters, including a picture of the ATLAS detector (an enormous particle detector at the Large Hadron Collider at CERN that particle physicists all around the world were using to search for the Higgs boson and supersymmetric particles), and a large detailed sketch of the ATLAS detector's cross section, showing all of its electrical components and how they worked together. Taped to the walls were news clippings about famous particle physics discoveries, jokes about bosons and string theory, and photographs of professors and graduate students standing around pieces of the ATLAS detector.

That morning, I met one of the research scientists in the particle physics group. He was leading many of the most interesting ATLAS electronics projects at Penn, and as he tried to explain some of them to me, I quickly got lost. When he asked if I had any experience with electronics, I was honest. "I don't know anything about electronics," I said, "but I'll learn. I promise I'll learn so quickly, and I will work so hard." My earnestness must have convinced him, because he hired me on the spot.

There were two different but related fields of experimental particle physics research: instrumentation, which was based on hardware, and analysis, which was based on software. First, you had to build the machines that would run the particle physics experiments—huge, dreadfully complicated machines with complex circuitry and customized electrical components. Second, you had to analyze the data that came from these machines, which required writing intricate algorithms that searched through terabytes of data, looking for new particles.

I started with instrumentation. My first hardware project entailed testing a set of special transistors. In order to decide whether to include these particular transistors in the ATLAS detector, the ATLAS Experiment needed to know if the devices could withstand intense radiation. We sent them off to several laboratories to be irradiated with protons; when they came back, I ran a series of tests on each of them to determine if they'd been damaged and whether they could successfully repair themselves through a process known as annealing. The researchers in the department mentored and guided me through the entire project. When the experiment was finished, and we knew which transistors could withstand the intense radiation of the ATLAS detector, the group decided to keep me on.

After that, I moved on to designing my very first electrical circuits and, soon after, I designed an entire circuit board that would eventually go into the ATLAS detector. Each circuit board had to be carefully designed and laid out—a process that I loved, in part because it was very similar to my childhood preoccupation with architecture. In each circuit, I had to decide where the electrical signals would go, what they needed to do, and what needed to be done to them. It was a bit like designing the layout of a building, and it was the most fun I'd had since those wonderful lazy days in my childhood, when I'd sit down with my drafting tools and draft paper and design buildings from scratch.

After I'd been working on instrumentation for a year, I wanted to give analysis a try. The leader of the experimental particle physics group offered me a project: rewriting an algorithm that would comb through some ATLAS data and determine the percentage of electrons that looked like photons in one of the searches for the Higgs boson. I'd never written a line of code in my life, and my code was pretty awful in the beginning. I didn't let myself get discouraged, though, because I knew from experience that I could pick anything up if I worked hard enough at it. I started working through free online coding classes at night, learning first the basics and then the intricacies of Python and C++. A few months later, I joined an ATLAS Experiment search for supersymmetric particles and became Penn's official representative in the group; I even had my name on some papers published within the ATLAS Experiment.

While I was working on analysis projects and taking my classes,

I kept working on hardware because it brought me so much joy, and I worked on various instrumentation projects almost every day until I left Penn three years later. My favorite hardware project was an electronics upgrade for the Roberts Proton Therapy Center, where patients with inoperable brain tumors like the one that had killed my father would go for "proton therapy"—a type of radiation therapy that entailed sending a carefully focused beam of protons straight into a patient's brain to kill the tumor while the patient wore a custom helmet that protected the rest of his brain from being irradiated. I designed and built a clock circuit board that kept all of the electronics synchronized, and helped our chief electrical engineer design and build a circuit board that monitored the position of the proton beam in real time to make sure that the beam was focused on the brain tumor.

Meanwhile, I was having the time of my life in my classes. The first few semesters of physics courses had been rough, and I didn't get the best grades, but I kept pushing through. As I learned more mathematics, my grades had gone from Ds and Cs to Bs and As. Now I was taking graduate courses in physics, studying everything from general relativity and liquid crystals to quantum mechanics and quantum field theory. I didn't let a single moment go to waste: whenever I wasn't doing my research or finishing up homework for my classes, I was studying extra topics like string theory and supersymmetry and spending countless hours talking to the theoretical particle physicists in the department.

It was a magical time in my life. I was on top of the world, and I'd never been happier. Thanks to my research and my classes, I felt like I finally understood the most fundamental workings of the universe in the way I'd always dreamed of. And in understanding it, I finally felt like I had found my place within the world.

By the spring of 2014, I was on track to graduate with three degrees: a BA in physics, a BA in philosophy, and an MA in philosophy. I couldn't believe how far I'd come. Over the last three years, I'd worked my way up from being a transfer student who had never taken a real math or physics course in her life to being on track to pursue a physics PhD and become a career physicist. I'd designed electronics for the ATLAS and CMS detectors, worked on a redesign of the electronics that powered the Roberts Proton Therapy Center at the Hospital of the University of Pennsylvania, and worked on a search for the Higgs boson and two types of supersymmetric particles at the LHC. As I prepared to apply for PhD programs that fall, I felt confident. I had good grades in my graduate courses, and I knew I wouldn't have a problem getting great letters of recommendation from professors in the department. I was so close to my dream that it already felt like a reality.

I had no idea it was all about to fall apart.

CHAPTER FOUR

At the end of the spring semester, a new student named Tim joined the department. He seemed to have trouble fitting in, so I reached out to him, hoping I could help him become part of the group. I'd been an outcast for most of my life, and now that I was a valued member of my research group and felt a sense of belonging, I wanted to help others who seemed to be having a hard time. I tried to befriend Tim. Whenever he was left out of conversations, I'd try to find a way to pull him in. Even though he worked on a different project and experiment than I did, whenever he was struggling with his code, I'd invite him to join me and some of the other students in my lab so we could help him.

One night, after several weeks of occasional conversation, Tim texted me a photo. In the photo, he was cutting one of his arms open, and his arm was bleeding. Horrified, I walked to his house, which was only a few streets away from my apartment, and sat down with him. I encouraged him to get help, gave him the phone number for the student counseling hotline, and offered to accompany him to the counseling center. He turned down my offer, and said he didn't want any professional help.

After that, I started walking on eggshells around Tim, because things only seemed to be getting worse. He was obviously having a mental health crisis; many things seemed to set him off and make him either harm himself or threaten to do so. When he started discussing suicide, I reached out to his advisor—a professor in the department—and explained that Tim was going through a serious mental health crisis, that his threats of suicide and self-harm were escalating, and that he refused to go to the counseling center. I was worried he was going to kill himself, and I didn't know what to do.

Initially, when we discussed the issue over the phone, Tim's advisor agreed that Tim needed professional assistance, and that this was far beyond anything I could help him with. After our call, I was relieved that Tim's advisor and the university would be stepping in. But then, later that same day, Tim's advisor asked me to meet with him and the outgoing chair of the department. Together, they explained that they wanted to help Tim, but they were afraid that if he knew I'd told them about his mental health crisis, he would harm himself or someone else. In their view, they said, Tim was now my responsibility: I was to persuade him to go to the counseling center (even if I had to drag him there), I was to give Tim's advisor daily updates on his mental health, and I was to stop doing my normal research work and focus on "helping" this student instead. "This is your job now," Tim's advisor told me.

I was stunned. They were putting both me and Tim in a terrible position. If I went along with their plan, I'd have to spend the

next God-knows-how-many-months trying to make sure an ac-
quaintance didn't harm or kill himself—something that wasn't fair
to Tim or to me. Without professional help, Tim might kill himself. For me, going along with their plan would also mean that I
would have to spend the time I normally spent on important physics research, studying for the GRE, and studying for my classes
helping Tim instead. If I didn't do as they said, I feared it could
jeopardize my future in physics: I was counting on several professors to write graduate school recommendation letters for me, and
without those letters, I knew I'd never get a PhD in physics.

At first, I told them I wanted nothing to do with it. Tim needed
professional help; I'd tried to get him professional help, and he
had refused it. When I said this, Tim's advisor and the chair of the
department called a number belonging to the City of Philadelphia; the person on the other line asked if I was willing to testify
that he was mentally unstable and have him committed to a psychiatric facility. I was horrified and confused. I believed that having Tim involuntarily committed to a psychiatric facility was not
my choice to make, or even a choice I should be involved in; it was
something that only Tim himself or an experienced mental health
professional should decide. So I refused, and the person on the
phone hung up. The message Tim's advisor and the department
chair were sending was clear: *Even the City of Philadelphia believes
you are responsible for Tim.*

They gave me a few minutes to make my decision. It wasn't
much of a decision. The school wasn't going to help Tim, and my
future was on the line. What was I supposed to do? What choice
did I have? I would be graduating at the end of the year, and I was

hopefully only a year away from starting graduate school. I couldn't put my future in jeopardy, and defying the professors in my lab and the chair of the department would do exactly that.

I decided to go along with their plan, to keep trying to help Tim and hope that things would get better. I accompanied him to the counseling center, spent time updating his advisor and other professors in the department about the state of his mental health, and put aside much of my own research work and coursework so that I could focus on helping Tim. Unfortunately, things only got worse. In the months that followed, Tim continued his threats of self-harm and suicide. When people in the department made a joke, or he didn't get a perfect grade on his homework, or he thought I was ignoring him, the threats would return. I started begging people in the department not to mention my name to him or joke around with him, because whenever they did, he would threaten to harm or kill himself. I begged Tim's advisor and other professors in the department to let me walk away from the situation, but they wouldn't.

One night, Tim told me that he had romantic feelings for me and asked me if I had feelings for him. When I told him that I didn't, he said he was going to kill himself. This time, it seemed real. I called the police. Once the police were on their way, I let Tim's advisor know that Tim had threatened suicide again and that I thought it was real this time. I explained that I'd called the police and that I didn't want to be involved in the situation anymore.

Tim was released from the hospital the next morning. According to him, the hospital judged that he hadn't actually tried to kill himself and wasn't a risk to himself or anyone else. He asked me to come over to his house because he didn't want to be alone. I didn't want to go, not after what had unfolded in the past twenty-four hours. I was scared of being around him, especially of being alone with him. "I know it's not about me," I texted Tim's advisor, "but I am so strained and exhausted. It's so rough having to be close friends with a fellow student/member of our research group just because I need to make sure he doesn't kill himself." He insisted I go to Tim's house and check on him anyway. I agreed, but I told him that this would be the last time. I was done, I was at the end of my rope. I didn't care anymore if the professors in the department were going to write letters of recommendation for me or not; at this point, my own sanity was on the line. When I saw Tim, he repeated what he'd told me the night before: he said that he was in love with me and that he wanted to kill himself because I didn't love him back.

I was a nervous wreck, afraid of going into work and school, afraid of being alone with Tim or even being around him, afraid of seeing my professors, because I knew that the professors in the physics department were angry at me. Tim's advisor and the outgoing chair of the department had told other people about the situation, and I'd met with other professors in the department—the ones who I had planned to ask for recommendation letters—who scolded me for my involvement in the situation. I felt like I was going crazy, because nothing that was happening made any sense. Why were they angry at me? What had I done wrong?

Meanwhile, the situation with Tim kept getting worse. When I reached out for help, and told the professors in the department that I didn't feel safe around Tim, the graduate chair of the physics department reiterated that I—not the physics department—was responsible for the situation. In response, I sent an email to the professors involved, summarizing all of the events of the past few months. "Guys, this is so messed up," I wrote. "I've been made to be responsible for making sure that *I* am safe. I have already rearranged my life to accommodate what I have been asked to do by the department to be responsible for [Tim's] mental health problems." Then I asked them, point-blank, "Can someone please explain to me why this is still my responsibility?"

The graduate chair replied, saying that "the department only has purview over academic issues and students' ability to finish their program. We are not health professionals or public safety officers and it is not our purview to handle these issues."

The situation dragged on into the summer. I again pleaded with Tim's advisor to let me off the hook, and proposed to him that I could send Tim an email explaining the whole situation; in the email, I proposed, I could tell him that he needed to stop relying on me and should start relying on Penn's counseling services for help with his mental health problems. (I wanted to send an email, rather than speaking to him about it in person, because I was afraid about how he would respond.)

I sent a draft of the email to Tim's advisor, and asked him if I could please send it to Tim. "This is so emotionally draining," I wrote in the email, "I don't know how much longer I can keep dealing with this." All I wanted was to send him the email and be done with it. Tim's advisor gave me suggestions for how to revise it; I sent him the revisions, but he asked me to hold off on sending it.

Tim's advisor then referred me to Penn's Women's Center, where the woman sitting across from me (who had clearly been briefed on the situation by Tim's advisor before our meeting) told me that the school wanted to help me, but they needed to prioritize helping "this young man." Another Penn student—a young track star named Madison Holleran—had killed herself earlier that year, and the school didn't want another suicide. Penn, the woman explained, was going to do everything necessary to keep Tim from killing himself. My presence in the lab, she said, was upsetting to Tim. My presence in classes, she said, was upsetting to Tim. She offered a two-part "solution": first, they'd move me to a different research group, and second, they would prohibit me from taking any of the classes that he wanted to take. I was livid. If I was moved to another research lab, I'd have to abandon the research that I'd been doing for the last two and a half years, research that was essential to my getting into graduate school; and if I couldn't take the physics classes in question, my graduate application wouldn't be very strong. There was even a chance I wouldn't be able to graduate with my physics degree.

I escalated the situation to the dean of graduate studies. I'd already met with her earlier that year, when I found out that the Penn philosophy department had neglected to file the paperwork for my master's degree in philosophy; at that time, she had assured me that she would follow up with the philosophy department and had promised I would graduate with the degree. When

I reached out to her about the situation with Tim, she seemed appalled, and wrote that she was "deeply concerned about what has been going on, and how it's been handled." In an email, she said that I should "lodge a formal complaint against the student," and that I could address the complaint to her in the Graduate Division and we could take it from there.

In late July, we met in her office, and she seemed very sympathetic.

"If I were you," she said, "I would sue the school. Is that what you want to do?" I shook my head.

"I don't want to sue anyone," I said. "I just want to graduate with all of my degrees and go to graduate school." I told her that I wanted to file two complaints: a complaint against Tim—for threatening to kill himself if I didn't reciprocate his romantic feelings—and a complaint against the school, for retaliating against me for reporting the harassment by prohibiting me from taking classes and trying to remove me from my research lab. She reiterated that any and all such complaints needed to be made through her, and asked me if I wanted her to file the complaint about Tim. I told her that I did, and she said that she would.

The conversation then pivoted to my master's degree in philosophy. Before I left, she assured me she would take care of everything, that she would make sure I could take the classes I needed, that she would make sure I could keep working in the physics department while no longer "being responsible" for Tim. She promised she would file the complaint about Tim, that the bad behavior would stop, and that I would receive my graduate degree.

As I stood up to leave, she stopped me and stood between me

and the door. "Are you sure you want to file a complaint against the university?" she asked. "Are you really sure?" I was confused as to why she was bringing this up after the whole conversation we'd just had, during which I'd made that very clear. I nodded. She said that she would look into the details of what filing a formal complaint against the university would entail, and opened the door. I left her office.

I was naive to believe her when she told me that she was the one who was supposed to file such complaints. In reality, because the complaints pertained to sex-based discrimination, they should have gone both to the school's Title IX coordinator and to the U.S. Department of Education. She never filed either complaint. And instead of helping me, she enacted further retaliation against me. She rescinded my master's degree in philosophy, on the grounds that I had withheld information from her, and mentioned some emails about my master's degree that she said I had "not included" in my documentation for her investigation. In her email about the situation, she said she hadn't filed any of the complaints we had discussed, and that, in fact, she wouldn't be doing so. "It is my hope that you can use this experience as fuel for getting your work done and moving on," she wrote.

I was completely shocked. Why was she taking my master's degree away, when she'd already promised I would graduate with it? And what did my master's degree have to do with Tim? In my response to her email, I explained that the emails in question—the ones she claimed I had withheld—"were sent to you, and were discussed quite clearly in our first meeting."

She didn't dispute any of this. All she said was that she would no longer discuss the situation with me. "When I said that case was closed, I really meant it," she wrote back.

It didn't add up. The dean was saying the school wouldn't award me the master's degree I had already earned (and paid for, using thousands of dollars in student loans I would now have to pay back over the next ten years), and her reason for doing so didn't make any sense. On top of that, she hadn't filed any of the complaints that she promised she would file. I remembered the way she had cornered me in her office after our meeting and asked me if I was *really sure* I wanted to file a complaint against Penn, and I wondered if she had in fact rescinded my master's degree in retaliation for trying to file the complaint. Reeling, I went to Tim's advisor and asked him why the dean had rescinded my degree, and his answer confirmed my suspicions. He said that the school had evidence that I had lied about my relationship to Tim. He said that I'd told them I wasn't in a relationship with Tim, but Tim had provided evidence to them that showed that this was a lie. Of course, when I asked to see this "evidence," the school refused to share it with me.

I then went to the Office of the Vice Provost, where I met with a woman who told me she "represented the provost." When I explained the situation, and asked for formal complaints to be filed against both the student and the university, she told me that this would not be possible. I was a student employee, not a "real employee," she said, and therefore I could not make *any* complaints about harassment, discrimination, or retaliation. Furthermore, she said that while "real employees" were protected by federal employment law, and were therefore protected against harassment, discrimination, and retaliation, there were no laws that protected me—a student—from harassment, discrimination, and retaliation. Instead of laws, she said, there were "learning opportunities," and a student in my position should view this as a "learning opportunity." Tim, Tim's advisor, the physics department, and Penn's administrative staff were viewing it as a "learning opportunity" for themselves, too, she said. The school, she explained, had issued a no-contact order against me (preventing me from contacting Tim or being near him), and had also given one to Tim; this, she said with an air of certainty, should be enough to protect me.

When I asked her what my options were if Tim contacted me despite the no-contact order, she said I didn't have any.

"Can I go to the police?" I asked.

"Yes," she said tentatively. Then she urged me not to go to the police, but to the Philadelphia District Attorney's office instead. The police, she said, wouldn't take my complaint seriously.

"Okay," I said, "then that's what I'll do." But I knew from experience that I wouldn't have to take such extreme measures, that the local police handled things quite differently from Penn's administration. Around the same time, a doctor who had recently been fired from Penn's student health services had started sending me sexually explicit messages on social media. I didn't even bother going to Penn administrators for help—I was justifiably afraid they'd try to find some way to spin it on me, try to make it my fault, even though it clearly wasn't my fault at all—and went straight to the police instead. At the police station, I spoke to two detectives, who assured me they would handle the situation and that, if needed, they'd help me obtain a restraining order. They then went and paid the doctor a visit, and he never contacted me again.

After my meeting at the Office of the Vice Provost, I did some research on the laws that existed to protect students from this kind of mistreatment and spent hours reading about Title IX. Before this, I'd known only the most basic facts about Title IX, a federal civil rights law that was created to protect students from sex-based discrimination. The more I read about it, the more I realized how insane the whole situation had become, realized that Penn had been gaslighting me the entire time. *Of course* there were laws that protected me from the treatment I was experiencing; Penn just didn't want me to know about them. That night, I laughed at myself until I had tears in my eyes—laughed at myself for believing the dean of graduate studies when she said she'd file the complaints on my behalf, for believing the Vice Provost's Office when they said I had no recourse.

The next day, I shared a post on my private Facebook page about laws protecting students from sexual harassment and discrimination, without mentioning Penn. Right after I shared the post, the provost's representative called my cell phone and berated me for talking about Title IX and student protections. "There will be consequences for this!" she screamed at me.

Immediately after our phone call, I sat down at my computer and summarized the incident in an email, and sent it to the provost's representative who had just screamed at me over the phone. I wrote that what had just happened was "inappropriate and unacceptable . . . You told me you had seen my Facebook posts and began criticizing me. . . . That you even thought it appropriate to get your hands on my private correspondence, and then lecture me about it, is very upsetting." I gave her the chance to correct any misunderstandings I might have had about the incident, but, in her reply, she didn't disagree with anything I said. Instead, she said that I could always "file a complaint/grievance" about the situation—with her office.

Horrified, I contacted the local bar association, which referred me to a handful of civil rights lawyers. I spoke with several of them, and they all gave me the same advice: put everything into email, document everything, and back up all of your documentation because you will need proof of all of this *in writing*. Never use your student email to talk about the case because Penn has access to your student email account and will read all of it. Most important, they all said, *don't sue Penn*. "You have a great case against Penn," one lawyer said, "but believe me when I tell you that you do *not* want to sue them, not when you are this young, not with your whole life ahead of you. You will be embroiled in this lawsuit for the next two to five years, and I promise you it's not worth it. Walk away."

I took the lawyers' advice and decided to move on with my life. But before I did, I carefully documented everything, saving every email, every call log, every text message. There was part of me that wondered if perhaps I'd change my mind about suing them in the future. And there was another part of me that thought I'd want to write about it someday. My heart broke when I realized that moving on meant giving up on my dream. The professors I'd been counting on for letters of recommendation now refused to talk to

me because of the situation with Tim, and without the recommendation letters I needed, I knew I would never be accepted into a
physics PhD program. So I trashed my graduate school applications and, with them, my hopes of becoming a physicist.

In the years since, I've become much more conscious of the weight
of my decision, and there have been many times when I've deeply
regretted backing away from the situation with Penn. I'd worked
so hard to get where I was, and I was very good at what I did, but
I let them take it all away without putting up much of a fight. Even
worse, I felt an enormous amount of guilt because I knew that I
had done the wrong thing. Going along with their plan was objectively wrong. It was wrong for me, and it was wrong for Tim; it was
wrong for so many reasons, and I *knew* it was wrong. I gave in
because I was afraid, but I knew in my heart that my fear didn't
absolve me of my moral responsibility.

When I reflect on what happened, I see two different paths I
could have taken. If I had given in to Penn's intimidation tactics
much earlier in the process, perhaps I could have obviated the
need for them to retaliate against me. I could have agreed to switch
research groups that fateful semester in order to avoid interacting
with Tim, just as they wanted me to. I could have agreed not to
take the same classes that he was taking. If I had done all of these
things, there's a chance that I would be at Caltech or Cornell or
the University of Arizona right now, finishing up a PhD in physics.
This scenario would have produced the outcome I wanted, but I
still would have done the wrong thing.

Or, I could have done the opposite: I could have refused to let them intimidate me from the very beginning; I could have said no and fought back. The very moment that they started to retaliate against me for not going along with their plan, I could have hired a lawyer, or I could have gone to the press and shared my story with the world. Looking back, I believe that was the objectively right thing for me to do. And I wish with all of my heart that I had done it.

Since leaving Penn, I've met many women who have experienced similar mistreatment in academic departments. Not all of these women were in physics, and not all of their stories involved harassment from a fellow student, but all of them experienced cruel and irrational retaliation from their school, and none of the schools suffered any consequences. To this day, I feel a pang of guilt on my conscience whenever I hear these stories. I wonder what would have happened if I'd decided to fight Penn in court, if I'd decided to take my story public. Could I have helped shed light on the awful ways that some universities and colleges silence and retaliate against their students? Would sharing my story have improved the lives and careers of women all over the world? I'll never know. All I know is this: I didn't speak up, because I was afraid. I didn't do what I knew was right, because I was afraid. And I vowed that I would never make the same mistake again.

Until everything fell apart, I had been certain that I was going to get a PhD in physics and eventually become a physicist, but now that I didn't have the letters of recommendation I needed, a PhD was out of the question. Teaching philosophy at a community college or small liberal arts college had been my backup plan, but without a master's degree in philosophy, that door was also closed to me. To my complete surprise, I now found myself in the same position as many of my graduating classmates: I was about to graduate, and I didn't know what to do next.

I was back at square one. I had no job, no career, and no idea what I was going to do with my life. I started to feel the way I had when I was a teenager back in Yarnell, without any direction, completely on my own. In the story of my life, I had once again become the object rather than the subject.

I started telling myself the same thing I used to tell myself when I was a kid, whenever I would get depressed: I was going to do great things; I was going to *be* great, and I wasn't going to let myself settle for anything less. I knew that I had to take control of my life and find a job after graduation. The new job didn't have to be my dream job or my calling; it just had to be the next step in my life. I felt overwhelmed, and had no idea what kind of jobs I should even apply for, so I reminded myself that I wasn't walking into the process empty-handed: I had a degree in physics from an Ivy League school, I knew how to code, and I'd built electronics for particle detectors. I said these things over and over to myself, hoping and praying for an answer, until it finally hit me: *I knew how to code.*

The answer had been staring me in the face for months, if not years. The entire time I'd been a student at Penn, I'd watched as my undergraduate classmates in both physics and philosophy interviewed with companies like Facebook and Google, did software engineering internships in San Francisco over the summers, and boasted about their high-paying job offers from companies like Palantir and Microsoft. Almost all of the graduate students in my physics lab left academia after they completed their PhDs or finished their postdocs and moved to New York or San Francisco to work as data scientists, software engineers, and product managers. Jumping from physics into the technology industry wasn't a very big leap: physics was a technical field, and physics students were technically inclined, comfortable with mathematics and computer science.

I suspected that the leap from physics into software engineering wouldn't be that difficult for me. Because I already knew how to code, the only things I'd need to figure out in order to qualify for a job were the basics of computer science. I considered taking a few months off after graduation and moving back in with my family in Arizona while I prepared for interviews, but I realized that I didn't have the time: I didn't have any money, and I had bills to pay.

I decided to jump in right away and figure things out as I went along. I was scheduled to graduate in December 2014, and I needed a job within one to two months after graduation, so, over the next several months, as I finished up my very last classes at Penn, I found myself swept up into a circus of job interviews. I was grateful for the chaos; it distracted me from the pain I felt about losing my future in physics and philosophy. I was wined and dined by Facebook, and did round after round of technical interviews with Google, picking up the basics of how software engineering jobs and tech companies worked as I went.

It didn't take me long to figure out that I didn't belong at a large company like Facebook or Google or an old and established company like IBM or Goldman Sachs, where I wouldn't have much individual responsibility or autonomy. I'd been largely in charge of my own day-to-day research and work for the past three years, and I didn't want to lose that. From the moment I learned about startups—which, in 2014, had a relatively good reputation for disrupting existing industries with innovative solutions, working harder and smarter than established companies, and being a bit out of the box—I knew that I wanted to work at one.

When I started interviewing with startups, I wasn't disappointed: at each company, I had at least one interview with the founders, and I loved hearing their passion for the work they were doing and the company they were building. My favorite was a phone interview with Chad Rigetti, the CEO and founder of a three-person quantum computing startup called Rigetti Quantum Computing, which was based in Berkeley, California. Chad was a physicist who was building computers that harnessed the power of quantum mechanics. At the time, quantum computing was still largely a theoretical and academic field; most people (including people at Penn) didn't believe that what Chad wanted to do—build commercially useful quantum computers—was possible. But he believed it could be done, so he started a company whose mission was to build the world's most powerful computers. I couldn't believe that there were opportunities to solve these kinds of scientific problems outside academia, and the company was solving one of the hardest scientific and engineering problems out there. I was hooked.

I really wanted the job at Rigetti Quantum Computing. It seemed perfect for me. But much to my dismay, the company never scheduled a second interview. I was sure there must have been a misunderstanding, because my call with Chad had gone so well, but after a few weeks I gave up and moved on.

Several days before Christmas, I flew out to California for my final on-site interview with another company in the San Francisco Bay Area—a twelve-person financial technology startup called Plaid—and was offered the job.

Even though I liked the company and knew I should probably accept the offer, part of me faltered at the last minute. I hadn't given much thought to the prospect of being a software engineer— I was in desperate need of a job after graduation, and this seemed like the only viable option—and I wondered if I was making a huge mistake. While I'd dreamed of becoming a violinist, an architect, a writer, a physicist, and a philosopher, I'd never felt that being a software engineer was my calling. And I didn't believe that being a software engineer was how I would accomplish great things or *be* someone great. I worried that by accepting the job, I would be giving up on my dreams—my dreams of writing, of designing houses, of discovering the nature of the universe, of figuring out how to live a meaningful life.

As I mulled over the offer, I reflected on my father's life. He never achieved his career dreams or did all the things he knew he was capable of; all his life, he worked jobs that he didn't love in order to support our family. But his life was still wonderful and precious, filled with love and joy. The thought occurred to me that if I could find a way to have a similar life, to find love and joy despite it all, then I would still have a pretty spectacular time here on Earth. And maybe, just maybe, I would find something bigger in San Francisco; maybe all of my wildest dreams would come true.

I worked up my courage and accepted the job, then started to get excited about it. I was determined to have fun and find joy in my new life, even if it wasn't the life I'd been planning and hoping for.

Saying goodbye to Penn was bittersweet. I felt terribly sad walking through the halls of the David Rittenhouse Laboratory for the last time, saying farewell to the professors, researchers, graduate students, and undergraduates who had changed my life. I tried my best not to let the bad experiences eclipse the good, because there was just so much good that had happened in those halls. They were the same halls where I'd chased down Ed Witten to ask him about B-L symmetry and proton decay; the same halls I'd walked on my way to the offices of my favorite professors, where they'd sit patiently with me for hours and hours, explaining quantum field theory and supersymmetry and cosmology until I finally understood; the same halls I would run down after making an important discovery that I wanted to share with my research team. I loved that building, I loved the things I had learned there, I loved physics, and, dear God, I loved the universe. More than anything, I loved very dearly the people who taught me everything I knew about physics and mathematics; I would miss them terribly, and I would forever be deeply grateful for everything they had given me.

As I walked out the side door of DRL for the very last time, I was struck by the realization that Penn had robbed me of more than just my degree, more than just my future in physics and philosophy. The most cruel thing the school had done was associate my name with fear and legal issues and harassment in the minds of the people who, before the incident with Tim, had been my mentors, my teachers, and my friends. After everything that happened that summer, many of the same people who used to love to talk to me about physics now avoided me. The same people who used to open their doors to me now kept them shut and ignored me. They were afraid of me. They were afraid of the whole situation. To them, I was no longer "Susan," the student they loved to teach, the weird girl who used to borrow their books, the excited young fledgling physicist who would sit in their offices and talk for hours about cosmic strings and quantum loop gravity and perturbation theory; now I was nothing more than a liability. I didn't blame them; it was easy for me to imagine how scared they must have felt. They didn't want to deal with a harassment complaint, and I don't think they even knew how to handle one. They just wanted to do their jobs; they just wanted to do physics. I wished I could tell them that I understood, that I didn't want to deal with it either, that I just wanted to do physics, too. And that was the most devastating feeling in the world.

I was glad to leave it all behind.

On the last day of January, after a couple of weeks at home with my family, I packed all of my belongings into my new Jeep Wrangler and drove from my mom's house in Wickenburg, Arizona, to the San Francisco Bay Area, where my new job as a platform engineer at Plaid was waiting for me.

CHAPTER FIVE

Looking back at it now, you could say that working at Plaid was a hazing ritual for working in Silicon Valley. It was a stereotypical small technology startup in every way, the kind of half company, half frat house immortalized in the show *Silicon Valley*. Plaid's founders, Zach and William, were two twentysomethings from well-to-do families who'd written their software application, which aggregated financial data, after graduating from college. They entered their app in the infamous TechCrunch Disrupt competition and won. When I joined the company, they'd just raised their Series A round of funding. I was the thirteenth or fourteenth employee.

When I walked into the office on my first day, I felt like I was part of something special, something fun. It was a tiny company, and all of my new coworkers—who were around the same age as I was—seemed genuinely excited about what they were working on. The office was far nicer than anything I'd ever seen, occupying a beautiful corner office of an older building in the heart of San

Francisco's Financial District, with two double rows of custom-designed wooden desks on one side of the office and a pool table on the other. I'll never forget the way I felt in that moment. *This is going to be an exciting ride*, I thought to myself. I had no idea just how wild it was going to be.

Everyone went out for drinks that night to celebrate the two new employees: me and the new office manager, Heidi. We were the only women in the office; as I later learned, they had us start on the same day so that we wouldn't feel "alone." I was the only woman in the office in a technical role (the only other technical woman, a data scientist, lived and worked in Boston), but that didn't seem strange or unusual to me; at Penn, I had been the only woman on the floor where my lab was located in the David Ritten-house Laboratory, and there were only men's bathrooms on the floor where I worked.

As the happy hour came to an end, we all stood outside the bar while each person called an Uber ride home. Zach, Plaid's CEO, helped me sign up for an Uber account and showed me how to request a ride on the app.

I'd only ridden in an Uber once before, on the night of Hallow-een just a few months earlier. Dressed as Princess Leia, I'd been bar hopping around Philadelphia with my friend Matt and his roommate Andrew. The last bar on our list had just closed, and we were trying to make our way back to Matt and Andrew's apart-ment, which was a few miles away. We'd been standing outside in the chilly October air trying to hail a cab for nearly half an hour and weren't having any luck. We were about to give up on finding a taxi and make the long trek back to the apartment, when I spotted a yellow cab approaching the corner across from us. I ran toward it in my white Princess Leia dress, waving my arms and hoping that my wig—which was barely hanging on to my head after many hours of dancing—would stay put. The cab sped off before I could get to it, and as it drove away, I noticed someone sitting in the backseat.

When I walked back to Matt and Andrew, I found the two of them huddled over Matt's phone, staring at the screen. "We're calling an Uber," Matt said, excitedly. He explained that Uber was an app that let you call a cab, but instead of a yellow cab, it was just a regular car, driven by a regular person instead of a taxi driver.

Within minutes, a dark gray car pulled up to the curb, and the three of us crammed inside. "Hey," I said, pulling on the sleeve of Matt's pilgrim costume, "what's this called again?"

"Uber!" he shouted. I tried to remember it, happy to have an option that seemed better than Philadelphia's unpredictable (and sometimes scary) yellow cabs, but I had completely forgotten its name until that night in San Francisco, at the end of my first day as a professional software engineer. I took my very first solo UberX ride that night, heading across the Bay Bridge to my Airbnb in Oakland, where I was temporarily staying until I could find an apartment.

I enjoyed living in the Bay Area and had fun taking BART to the city every morning to work. The weather was lovely, and it seemed as though there were so many interesting people everywhere doing so many interesting things. I went on long drives up and down Highway 1, exploring the beautiful coastline. I even took some flying lessons, stalling a small plane over the bay, staring out at the vast Pacific Ocean on the horizon. I loved my day-to-day job, fixing bugs and working with customers like Venmo, Coinbase, and Robinhood to address problems with their Plaid integrations. I got along well with my coworkers, and we always had a lot of fun: we built software together, ate together, played pool and cards together, and went out drinking together. Before long, my Plaid coworkers were some of my closest friends.

The work was difficult, and it took up nearly all of my time. I worked between twelve and fourteen hours each day (even on weekends), but in the beginning I didn't mind. I was used to working hard, and there was a lot to learn. I loved all the new things I was learning. In addition to getting comfortable with new programming languages like JavaScript, I was learning about the tech industry itself: about fundraising and venture capital firms (everyone jokingly referred to a local sandwich place called "Andersen's" as "Andreessen's" after the famous venture capital firm Andreessen Horowitz), about how the startup ecosystem worked, and more. I loved every minute of it.

It certainly didn't hurt that for the first time in my life I was no longer poor. I was *almost* middle-class, and with that came a kind of emotional freedom and security that I'd never experienced before. I was still living paycheck to paycheck, but no longer had to overdraft my bank account and run up credit card debt; instead, I was finally able to start paying off my credit cards. I still had nightmares about not being able to buy food—recurring dreams that had plagued me since I was a young girl—but those night-mares never again became my reality. Instead of budgeting care-fully for food, I started buying more than I could ever possibly eat. I loved opening up the fridge and seeing rows of fresh fruits and vegetables, loved being able to try things that I'd never been able to justify buying before: the little plastic bins of precut fresh fruits, the expensive orange juice, the cage-free eggs, the antibiotic- and hormone-free meat.

Even on my decent salary, I still couldn't afford an apartment anywhere in the Bay Area. In what turned out to be a stroke of very good luck, I moved into another Airbnb in the East Bay: a bedroom in a big orange pumpkin of a house owned by Liz and Bob, a free-spirited, wonderful couple who took me in and made me feel like part of their family. Liz was a math teacher and dancer who, like me, loved books and art and music and science and mathematics. Bob had a lot of corporate experience, and was al-ways there when I needed advice about work and life. The house soon felt like home: whenever I had some free time, I played my violin in the living room, cuddled with their two fluffy cats, or sat down for dinner with Liz, Bob, and whoever was renting the other spare bedroom. What began as an Airbnb became my permanent Berkeley home, where I lived until I moved in with my fiancé al-most two years later.

During my time at Penn, I'd read something by the sociologist C. Wright Mills in which he had written, "The aim of the college, for the individual student, is to eliminate the need in his life for the college; the task is to help him become a self-educating man." When I first came across this, I thought back to my teenage years and the long nights I spent poring over every book I could find, trying to learn everything I could about the world. I'd never considered, in those days, that I would leave college and feel like I had barely scratched the surface of all of the things I wanted to learn. But, after I graduated, I found that there was so much I still wanted to know, so much more I wanted to learn: number theory, knot theory, ancient Egyptian art and history, condensed matter physics, mechanical engineering, archaeology, entomology—I wanted to understand it all.

I was delighted to discover that, thanks to all of the years I'd spent educating myself, both through high school and when I taught myself basic physics and math at Penn, learning was now a fully entrenched habit, ingrained in my framework for life. I created some fun "classes" that I taught myself, and pretended I was about to start a new semester at school, buying dozens of blank notebooks, a case of my favorite fine-point pens, and a handful of math, philosophy, and foreign-language textbooks. Each evening, I would cozy up in my bed with one of the cats, spread my notebooks and textbooks across my blue floral quilt, and study late into the night until I fell asleep. In those early days at Plaid, there were so many mornings when I woke up with my face in the set theory or ancient philosophy book I'd been studying the night before.

The one thing in my life that wasn't going very well was dating. After moving to the Bay Area, I went on a string of first dates that went absolutely nowhere. Some of them were comically disastrous: there was the guy who told me that he never showered or used soap because he was trying to cultivate his "biome"; there was also the guy who asked me out after seeing me reading a computer science book on BART, then told me that if I wanted to date him, I'd need to stop being so nerdy and learn how to dance and have fun going out on the town. In addition, it seemed that all the men and women my age were interested only in hooking up or being in "open" relationships, but neither of these options were appealing to me. I didn't want hookups, casual relationships, or polyamory; I didn't want modern love with its convenience, emotional distance, and practicality. I was an old-fashioned romantic idealist, and what I wanted was intense, lasting, almost-fairy-tale, monogamous love. Friends, potential suitors, and exes made fun of me and told me it didn't exist, but I had seen it, and I knew it was real. My mother and father had it: they were soulmates, destined for each other; they loved each other wholly and completely and with all of their hearts, and they knew the moment they met that they were meant to be with each other. And I knew that kind of love wasn't just a relic from another time or for an older generation, because Shalon had recently gotten married, and she and her husband, Tristan, were soulmates too. I wanted that kind of great, wonderful, all-consuming love, and I wasn't going to settle for anything else.

After one particularly rough date, I sat down with my journal and resolved to give up on dating for the next few years. I listed off a few things I was determined to accomplish before I dated again: I'd finally become fluent in Ancient Greek, improve my violin and piano playing, understand everything in Steven Weinberg's three books on quantum field theory, and become a truly, genuinely good human being, holding myself to the highest standards. I was convinced that I wouldn't meet "the one" until I was the best possible version of myself, but I think the truth was I feared that if I met him or her before I was the best possible Susan, I might not be good enough.

After a few months at Plaid, things took a turn. It started to feel a lot more like a continuation of the college environment than a professional workplace. There was something about it all—the free clothing, the free food, the constant drinking, the expensive parties—that didn't feel quite right to me. I'd never worked a corporate job before, but I began to suspect that this wasn't how things were supposed to be. It wasn't just Plaid, however; this seemed to be true for most companies in Silicon Valley. When I asked other engineers about workplace culture at tech companies, many of them boasted that the lack of normal corporate professionalism was what made working in Silicon Valley so much fun. I agreed it was fun, but only up to a certain point. When the companies gave employees everything they "needed" in life—friends, a social life, food, and more—at the office, they made it difficult for those employees to have autonomy and build lives of their own. As time went on, I started to fear that my life was being completely consumed and dictated by my day job, and that my autonomy and independence were slowly diminishing.

In the spring, I was put on call for Plaid's software systems, which meant I was the only engineer besides the system administrator who was responsible for responding immediately if the system went down, at any time of the day or night. I'd already been working twelve- to fourteen-hour weekdays and working every single weekend, but now I had to wake up in the middle of the night to fix code. Whenever one of the banks would block Plaid's software from accessing its servers, my pager would go off and I'd wake up, pull my laptop into bed, and hack away at the code until it worked again.

I was no longer sleeping through the night, and I soon began to worry that the demands of the job were taking a toll on my mental and physical well-being. I wanted to work fewer hours, just like the rest of the employees. When I brought this up with William, Plaid's CTO, however, he said it was unacceptable for a junior engineer to work less than twelve hours a day and that he needed to see me online even on Saturdays and Sundays. I hadn't proven myself as an engineer, he said, and he wouldn't treat me like one until I worked even harder.

I knew working like this wasn't sustainable. And, as far as I could tell, I was the only one who was working this way; none of the other engineers appeared to be fixing the bugs in the critical production systems that extracted data from the banks, and nobody else except the sysadmin was on call or worked the same long hours and over weekends. One day, I overheard some of my male coworkers discussing their salaries, and I learned that they were making around fifty thousand dollars more each year than I was, even though they worked fewer hours. With this knowledge in hand, and the confidence that came from knowing that I was performing a crucial service for the company by keeping the production systems running, when my summer performance review rolled around, I asked William for a raise. He denied my request, saying that I needed to prove my dedication to the company before I "deserved" a raise.

I realized then and there that I wasn't valued at Plaid, and so I quit, six months after I had begun. I was sad to be leaving the company; I'd gotten quite close with many of my coworkers, and I knew I would miss working side by side with them every day. But I desperately needed more free time, less stress, more autonomy, and more money. Despite how much I'd been working, I was still living paycheck to paycheck, and I needed to start paying off the many tens of thousands of dollars in student loan debt that I'd graduated with.

When looking for my next job, I made sure to ask people I knew about good job opportunities. Unfortunately, with how much I'd been working, I didn't have many friends in the Bay Area aside from my Plaid coworkers. And while I'd heard a lot about the so-called whisper networks that purportedly helped women in Silicon Valley avoid workplaces where they might encounter discrimination, harassment, and other forms of mistreatment, I didn't have access to any such networks. "You have to be *somebody*" to be part of those networks, one woman who worked in venture capital told me; as far as the whisper networks were concerned, I was a nobody. I applied for jobs at a few of the larger, famous startups but never heard back.

Then, one day, one of my friends at Plaid told me about a startup called PubNub. He said he used to work with one of its engineering managers and really liked him. I was excited to hear good things about a company from someone I trusted, and when

I started looking into it, I found that PubNub was working on something that interested me quite a bit: building out publish-subscribe messaging as a service. Whenever a company needed to send mobile notifications or messages to its customers, it needed to build this software capability up from scratch, something that wasn't very easy to do. PubNub made it simple, offering a sort of plug-and-play model for sending out notifications. Hundreds of companies used PubNub, including Twitter's newest acquisition, a live-streaming social video company called Periscope. The technology was interesting to me; plus, in the role the company was looking to fill, I wouldn't have to be on call. I would have a normal work schedule, would have more time to learn and read and play the violin, and maybe even have time to make friends outside of work.

I liked PubNub's operations team when I interviewed with them, and when the offer came in, the salary was much higher than what Plaid had been paying me. For good measure, I googled PubNub to see if I could find anything negative, but I didn't come across any red flags, so I accepted the offer.

I've always approached each change in life as a chance to reinvent, redefine, or improve myself. When I started at Plaid, I had a long list of things that I wanted to do better, old habits I was going to break, and new habits I was going to make. When I left Plaid and started at PubNub, I made myself a new list, determined to re-make myself yet again. A few days before I started my new job, I resolved—just as I had at Plaid—to use every minute at work to be productive, to learn, and to be the best I could be; this time, however, my highest priority was having a good work-life balance.

My time at PubNub got off to a great start. I loved the infrastructure challenges and had a blast figuring out how to spin up new virtual data centers in the cloud. But while the technology was fun, I soon discovered that I didn't have much in common with my coworkers, and things got weird rather quickly. At every company all-hands meeting, the CEO and CTO would stand in front of the company and proclaim they were going to be bigger than Facebook, bigger than Google, and all of the employees would shout and cheer in agreement. When employees were told that Ashton Kutcher and Jared Leto were going to invest in the company, meetings were no longer about the technology but about how amazing PubNub must be now that it was about to have celebrity investors. I understood that they were trying to encourage their employees, but it seemed like a really big stretch to me. The company had a great service, and it was growing, but they were obviously never going to be the next Google or Facebook; as far as I was concerned, that was *okay*, but they didn't seem to think so.

Once again, I was the only woman on the engineering team. When I joined, I didn't think this was strange, because the company was still pretty small. But as time went on and the company hired more male engineers, I started to wonder if there was a reason besides statistics that the company didn't have any other female engineers.

Within a few days, I found out that my boss—who managed me and one other employee—was openly, unabashedly sexist. He commented on my clothing, making fun of me if I ever dressed nicely and telling me I was dumpy if I wore jeans and a T-shirt. He told me that he bet any man I was dating was off secretly having sex with prostitutes. He was also anti-Semitic, frequently commenting about how "stingy" and "Jewish" he thought the founders were (I didn't dare tell him that I was Jewish, too). The only way I could deal with it was to keep my head down, do my work, and try not to pay attention to anything he said. To keep myself sane, I read the philosophers Epictetus, Seneca, and Marcus Aurelius every morning on my way to work and during my lunch breaks.

Around a month into my new job, I was walking down the street with my manager and several other employees on our way to get lunch. As we approached an intersection, the light turned red, and we stopped alongside a mother pushing her adorable, sleeping baby in a stroller. I said hello to her and commented on how cute her baby was. After the light turned green and we walked away, my manager turned to the other engineers and pronounced that all women were the same. We were all "just like" his wife: we tricked men into thinking we cared about careers and education, tricked them into thinking we were worth all the training and money that men were worth, when we really just wanted to raise babies and leech their money off them. As he continued to rant, it became abundantly clear that this man truly, deeply, passionately hated women.

I'd encountered many different forms of discrimination over the course of my life. When I was a very young girl, I stumbled on a white supremacist meeting with a friend as we were exploring her neighborhood. White supremacism and anti-Semitism had been sweeping through our town like wildfire, something my father bravely stood at the pulpit every Sunday and denounced. In the weeks that followed, my sleep was plagued with nightmares; I was certain that they had seen me—after all, I'd been close enough to see them—and I was terrified that the white supremacists and neo-Nazis would come for our family. When I was a teenager and I would go out for dinner with the girls I was dating, we knew that, especially in the rural, conservative area where we lived, we could be mocked, bullied, assaulted, or even killed for what we were doing. When I was older and several graduate students and postdocs in the Penn physics department suspected that I dated both men and women, I was publicly humiliated and degraded; in one instance, a man in the department used a string of homophobic insults to describe me to other physicists in our research group. I'd also encountered my fair share of class-based discrimination at Penn. During my three years at the school, I was called "white trash" by fellow students, and along with other students who came from lower-class families, I often couldn't participate in programs offered by the school (including extracurricular programs), because they required students to pay for things out of pocket that weren't covered by financial aid.

I'd also been targeted because of my sex. When I was a young teenager, working as a nanny and babysitter, I'd had to deal with inappropriate behavior from some of the children's fathers. The creepy ones would attempt to flirt with me, asking me inappropriate sexual questions; the worst tried to force themselves on me, and one of them violently assaulted me. And when I was seventeen,

I worked at a retail store in which the manager would constantly and creepily attempt to flirt with me; one day, he didn't show up at work, and my coworkers and I learned he'd been imprisoned for statutory rape. As horrifying as these experiences I had were, they were nothing unique where I came from: every teenage girl I knew had experienced similarly disgusting treatment.

Long before I started working as a software engineer, I had grown accustomed to fear, accustomed to hate. I was used to people hating me and mistreating me because of my Jewish background, for my sex, for my sexual orientation, for my social class. I didn't understand it; I couldn't figure out why people harbored so much hatred in their hearts. As a teenager, I'd believed with all of my heart that if I made it out of poverty, if I worked hard enough and got what I called a "fancy, high-paying job," I'd never have to endure that kind of treatment again, because I believed that the creepy, inappropriate, demeaning, and discriminatory treatment I'd experienced came from a place of profound ignorance— that the people who held so much hatred in their hearts only did so because they didn't know any better. After what happened at Penn, I told myself that things would be better outside academia, in the "real world"; I believed that the treatment I'd experienced at the school happened because there were not enough laws in place that protected students against mistreatment. But now I had that "fancy, high-paying job" in the real world—one that I'd assumed would earn me a little more respect, one that was ostensibly protected by hefty federal employment law—and it seemed like things weren't all that different.

The thought that such treatment might follow me, no matter

how high up the socioeconomic ladder I climbed, absolutely terrified me. And as I listened to my manager at PubNub openly speak
hateful words about me and other women, I realized that he hated
me for the one thing I couldn't hide. I'd learned to keep my Jewish heritage invisible, my sexual preferences hidden; I'd learned to
pretend I didn't come from a town full of trailer parks, to cover
my tattoos, to carefully study books on manners so I would fit into
society. But how was I ever going to hide the fact that I was a
woman?

I had never defined or judged myself by any of the characteristics that people used to discriminate against me, like my sex or my
ethnicity. I wanted to be judged not for arbitrary properties about
myself that I couldn't change, but by the kind of person that I was:
by my work and accomplishments, by my character. By seeing me
as nothing but a representative of my sex, my manager had robbed
me of that. Worse still, I realized with horror, this jerk was my
boss, responsible for my career development, my performance reviews, and my pay. His bias could have a serious adverse effect on
my career—and the careers of other women on his team, if they
ever hired any—and I couldn't allow that.

Until that point, I'd avoided reporting him. I didn't want to
become a victim of the situation; I didn't want to be branded the
woman who was harassed, or the troublemaker, or the "problem"—
or whatever else they would say about me—as I had been at Penn.
I didn't want to be seen as a liability rather than as the hardworking employee I was. But now I felt I had no choice: I needed to say
something.

In order to report his behavior, I tried to find a human resources

representative at the company. But, as it turned out, PubNub didn't
have an HR department; the person who handled HR-related complaints was the company's general counsel. Because of my experience at Penn, I knew that talking to the company's lawyer was
probably not a good idea. Penn had a place where students could
go for legal advice, and when the school was retaliating against
me and refusing to grant me the master's degree, I had asked for
their help, wrongly assuming that they were there to give students
legal advice about situations having to do with Penn, when, in reality, it appears they existed to help Penn students get out of legal
trouble they had gotten into on or off campus. After I told them
my story, they said they would be representing Penn—not me—in
any lawsuit I brought against the school. Because of this, I knew it
would be a mistake to go to PubNub's lawyer. I didn't know who I
should ask for help. I felt trapped. I wanted to leave the company,
but I knew that I'd have a hard time explaining to future employers
why I'd lasted only six months at my first job and far less than that
at my second. I made up my mind that I would do whatever I
needed to do to survive there for one full year and then move on—
and maybe even leave science, technology, and Silicon Valley behind forever.

I'd been working at PubNub for just two months when an engineering manager from Uber reached out to me on LinkedIn and
asked if I wanted to join the world's fastest-growing startup. The
opportunity couldn't have come at a more perfect time. My manager's sexist behavior was only getting worse, and on top of that he

and another engineering manager had picked a fight over engineering responsibilities, and the engineering and infrastructure
groups were locked in a pointless political battle. The power
struggle exhausted me and my coworkers, and the atmosphere in
the office was one of fatigue and dread.

I was excited to hear from Uber. Over the past eight months in
San Francisco, I'd noticed that Uber was everywhere. Everyone I
met used Uber, and after every meeting or party or bar outing,
and at the end of every night, all I would hear was "Did you call
your Uber?" "Can I call you an Uber?" and "Is that your Uber or
mine?" It seemed as if half the cars on the street were being driven
by Uber drivers. Uber was ubiquitous, its name synonymous with
hailing a ride-share, a complete replacement for the old world of
standing on the curb waving down yellow taxicabs.

It felt strange to me at first—getting into a stranger's car, trust-
ing that this regular person in his regular car had both the driving
skills and the experience to safely take me where I needed to go—
especially after spending the last three years hailing yellow cabs in
Philadelphia. I initially used the Uber app sparingly. But when I
hurt my foot running on the sidewalks of Berkeley in the spring
and found myself needing to get to the North Berkeley BART station while on crutches, I finally caved and started using Uber as
one of my primary methods of transportation.

Whenever I found myself with talkative drivers, I'd ask how
they liked driving for Uber. The majority seemed happy. Many of
them had picked it up after retirement, some because they needed
extra cash, others because they were bored and wanted something
to do. Others drove as a full-time job, staying on the road for long

stretches, pulling eight- to twelve-hour days. I met a stay-at-home mom who homeschooled her children during the day and drove at night, after her husband came home, so that she could earn some extra cash and talk to adults after spending her days with her kids. I met a man who had recently been homeless, who used to dig old soda and beer cans out of trash bins and recycle them in order to buy food; he was able to lease a car and drive for Uber and was no longer living on the streets. I met college students who drove during their breaks. All of the Uber drivers had one thing in common: they all seemed to love driving for Uber. A picture of Uber's role in society began to form in my mind, and I started to really like this strange ride-sharing company.

Even so, at first I thought it would be best to ignore the message from Uber. I didn't want to look like a job-hopper, and even though my job was rough, the rest of my life was filled with joy. I had a busy, full social life: I spent a great deal of time with my friends from Plaid, my younger sisters flew out from Arizona to see me, and many of my old friends traveled to San Francisco from Philadelphia and Arizona just to visit me. I'd started taking violin lessons again and practiced every night for several hours. I studied logic and set theory and spent my daily commute to San Francisco listening to Russian and German language-learning tapes, just as my father had. I even revived my old dream of becoming a writer and wrote a novel about the modern American West. I made a note to myself that I would apply for a job at Uber as soon as I was close to the one-year mark at PubNub, and tried not to think too much about the fact that I had another ten months to go.

Then, one day in the early fall, my manager told me that the company had installed hardware inside the office that would allow them to read their employees' SMS text messages. I was sure he was joking, until one of the directors of engineering showed me the details of the hardware they used. Multiple engineering directors confirmed: the director of DevOps, the director of the external API software, the director of IT. My boss joked that he was looking forward to reading all the intimate text messages I sent to anyone I was dating.

That was the last straw. I got a new phone, never connected it to the company Wi-Fi, refused to install any of the company's security certificates on it, and kept it off during work hours.

As soon as my new phone was set up, I agreed to a phone interview with Uber.

CHAPTER SIX

My first interview with Uber went remarkably well. The manager I spoke to, Eamon, was enthusiastic about his job and about Uber. At the end of our call, he asked me to come into the office for an in-person, on-site interview.

Before my interview with Eamon, I'd spent a lot of time searching online for things like "Uber sexual harassment," "Uber discrimination," and "Uber work culture," determined to avoid a repeat of my past experiences. But nothing bad came up: from the Google search results, it looked like Uber had never been sued by its employees. I was relieved, taking this to mean that it had a good work culture. It made sense, I thought; a company as big as Uber probably couldn't get away with what happened at smaller companies, because the story would eventually get out.

What I didn't know at the time was that the mere fact that there was no public record of wrongdoing wasn't because Uber had a spotless record, but because all Uber employees were bound by forced arbitration. Forced arbitration clauses are often included

in employment agreements that workers must sign as a condition
of employment, usually on their very first day of work—not only at
tech companies like Uber, but at many companies in the United
States.* Most employees aren't aware of what they are agreeing to
when they sign these—the clauses are written in heavy legalese—
and rarely realize the consequences of signing such agreements
until it is far too late. Under forced arbitration, employees are
not allowed to sue their employers in open court if they experience mistreatment like harassment, discrimination, or retaliation.
Instead, any complaints are restricted to secret arbitration pro-
ceedings in which the arbitrator is bought and paid for by the
company. Almost every case of arbitration is accompanied by a
gag order, which prevents the employee from ever discussing his
or her mistreatment or the arbitration process with anyone.

I would later learn of multiple cases of retaliation or harassment or discrimination in which Uber employees were forced into
arbitration and legally prohibited from speaking about their experience. But, at the time, having done my due diligence and finding
nothing, I decided to move forward with the application process.
Much to my dismay, my on-site interview was delayed. After I
learned I'd made it past my phone interview, I waited a few days
and heard nothing back from Eamon or Uber's in-house recruiters. Days turned into weeks. Just when I was ready to write them

* Up to 80 percent of Fortune 500 companies use forced arbitration (http://employee
rightsadvocacy.org/publications/widespread-use-of-workplace-arbitration/), and an estimated 60.1 million employees in America are bound by forced arbitration agreements,
and cannot sue their employers in court (https://www.epi.org/publication/the-growing
-use-of-mandatory-arbitration-access-to-the-courts-is-now-barred-for-more-than
-60-million-american-workers/).

off, a recruiter named Carter reached out to me to schedule the interview. Uber was sorry for the delay, he said. They'd just returned from their company trip to Vegas, he explained, and had been too busy dealing with the fallout from that "crazy" trip to schedule interviews.

Unbeknownst to me, Carter's description of the Vegas trip as "crazy" was a serious understatement. After my blog post came out, *The New York Times* ran an investigation into Uber's culture, and reported that the Vegas trip had been an incredibly extravagant—and debauched—company gathering. Uber's CEO, Travis Kalanick, had arranged for the entire company to fly into Vegas and party for a few days. There was unlimited alcohol, food, and entertainment. Beyoncé—who, along with her husband, Jay-Z, had invested in Uber—gave the employees a private concert. One of the employees stole a van. One of the male employees assaulted a female employee. Several employees were caught with drugs. One of my coworkers later told me that all of the employees who went on the trip were "drunk out of their minds," at every meeting, from early in the morning until late into the night, for the entirety of the trip.

What should have been a clear red flag to me (why would there be "fallout" from a company trip?) barely registered. At the time, I was too eager about the possibility of a new job—and too eager to leave PubNub—to see anything else clearly. I was constantly daydreaming about working somewhere that had a real impact on the world, at a company where people were excited to come into work and passionate about solving problems, a company that had an HR department, a company where my manager wouldn't say inappropriate things to me and joke about reading my personal text messages. And I wondered if this job at Uber could end up being more than just a job, if it could be the beginning of a real career in engineering.

While I counted down the days until my interview, I asked more Uber drivers about their experiences. I tried to pry from them the worst, most awful things they'd experienced or seen, but the worst thing they ever said about driving for Uber was that they were worried the company would cut fare prices to stay competitive with Lyft, its rival.

Uber's corporate headquarters was located at 1455 Market Street, a building it shared with Square and several other companies, but that wasn't its only office in San Francisco. Several BART stops northeast on Market Street, right off the Montgomery Street BART station, were Uber's two engineering offices. The precise locations of these unmarked offices were a strongly guarded secret at the time, allowing Uber employees and executives to work in relative anonymity—something I would come to understand the importance of when I saw anti-Uber protests and riots break out outside the doors of 1455, not too long after I joined the company.

My on-site interview took place in one of these secret engineering offices. Even though it was Uber's least glamorous office in San Francisco, it was by far the fanciest office I'd ever seen. I took the elevator up to the top floor, where I was greeted by a recruiting coordinator who gave me a short tour. Each floor was the same: there were rows of open desks, where engineers sat in front of large Apple monitors, and stylish sitting areas, where engineers sat on couches and chairs, typing on their laptops. Glass-walled conference rooms lined the interior and exterior walls. Each floor had a fully stocked kitchen with unlimited food, snacks, and drinks, she told me, and a few had cafeterias, where the employees gathered for breakfast, lunch, and dinner. Dinner, she pointed out, was served very late in the evening, which I soon learned was one of Uber's ways of encouraging people to stay late at work.

She led me into one of the glass-walled conference rooms facing into the building's central courtyard, which was (then and always) under construction. I sat there alone for a few minutes, at a gray plastic conference table surrounded by four gray plastic office chairs, awaiting my interviewer. There was a large television screen on one wall and a gigantic whiteboard on the other; I could see the shadows of old writing on the whiteboard, those ghostly green, black, blue, and red marks that you can almost, but not quite, read. I looked out into the offices, where several engineers were seated, staring at their dual monitors, eyes glued to their screens.

My first interview was with Eamon, the manager who had recruited me, and it was on my favorite topic: software architecture. It was a typical "architecture" or "design" interview, in which the job candidate is asked to design an app (sometimes an app like Foursquare, sometimes a program like Excel, sometimes even an app like Uber itself), pretending at first that it has only ten users. The candidate is expected to draw out the architecture of the app on the whiteboard, sort of like the architecture of a house, except instead of bathrooms and living rooms there are databases, load balancers that divide the traffic between servers, API endpoints, and the like. Then comes the tricky part. "Imagine," the interviewer would say, "that you now have ten thousand users instead of just ten—where would things start to break down, and how would you change the architecture of your system?" This is where the candidate is expected to get into the basics of building scalable distributed systems, into how software systems break and fail. Every type of technology has limitations—some things work well with millions of users, and other things don't—and it's every engineer's job to know those limitations and learn to work around them. The numbers of users only went up from there: What about a hundred thousand users? What about a million? On and on and up and up the interviewer would ask the candidates to scale the system, until they'd lost their minds with stress, run out of time, or been completely stumped.

This was where I excelled. I'd never worked on anything close to Uber's unprecedented computing scale, but I'd built scalable systems, and I knew what I was talking about. I thought the interview went very well, and I liked Eamon and wanted to work with him. Next was a nontechnical "culture" interview, in which the interviewers tried to figure out if I would be a good "culture fit" for Uber. Then came the first of two programming interviews, where instead of designing a software system, I had to write code.

While the employees and managers were interviewing me, I did my best to also interview them: What is the work-life balance like here at Uber, I asked, and what is *your* day to day like? How are failures handled? What are the biggest technical challenges and the biggest nontechnical challenges? Every answer sounded reasonable to me, and they were very effective at selling me on the benefits and merits of the job. The engineers seemed to love their work, enjoyed collaborating with others within the company, and had good work-life balance.

I never asked how many women they had on their teams, and I never had to. The interviewers all volunteered the information at the beginning of each interview, each of them saying the same thing: "Twenty-five percent of our engineers are women." I kept hearing this magical number repeated. One of my interviewers took it a step further. "We have more women," he said, "than Google, than Amazon—than all of the big tech companies, really." I loved the idea of working someplace where I wouldn't be the only woman, where I would—hopefully—be paid and treated equitably. I was sold.

The interviews zoomed by, and I soon found myself standing in front of the whiteboard for my final interview, a dry-erase marker in my hand. The interviewers asked me to solve a programming problem. I put the marker to the whiteboard and then paused. They asked me to solve the problem in the programming language of my choice, so I chose the language I knew best: C++. I started writing the solution on the board.

"What's that?" one of the interviewers asked. I paused again, realizing he was asking what programming language I was using to write the solution.

"Do you mind if I write the solution in C++?" I asked. They

glanced at one another and hesitated. I explained that I'd written most of my code in C++, and writing this particular solution in C++ would be more efficient.

"We don't know any C++," one of the interviewers said slowly.

"Ah," I said. "Okay. How about I write it in C++, and I'll explain the code to you as I go." They nodded. I began to solve the problem on the whiteboard, doing my best to explain the solution, and they seemed to follow along.

Before I left the building, I stopped by the restroom. While I was washing my hands, a member of the janitorial staff came in and began to clean. I watched her for a moment, feeling that there was something strange about the situation, but I couldn't figure out what it was. I walked back out into the hall, where the recruiting coordinator was waiting to escort me out of the building, and we made our way through the floor. As she led me past the same rows of desks and conference rooms we had passed on our tour, I still couldn't shake the feeling that there was something wrong, something *off* about the office. When we reached the elevator, it struck me: in each interview, the interviewer had made a point of emphasizing the large number of female engineers who worked on the teams, but the only women I could recall seeing during my visit were the recruiting coordinator and the janitor.

The next day, I received an email from Carter. Most of the people who interviewed me loved me, he said, but some of the interviewers had doubts about my programming abilities. In order to move forward, they needed me to work on a somewhat difficult take-home programming assignment, which they would then use to properly assess my coding abilities. I was a bit confused, because I thought I'd done quite well in the programming interviews, but agreed to complete the assignment.

When the programming assignment hit my inbox, I couldn't help but laugh: Carter had sent me the very first Project Euler problem to solve. Project Euler is one of the most popular programming websites for software engineers, computer science students, and math students; it's a series of mathematical problems for people to solve, ranging from extremely easy puzzles to problems that only a few people in the world have ever been able to solve. Saying that sending me the easiest Project Euler problem was an insult would be putting it mildly: it implied that I had no knowledge of computer science, of mathematics, that I was less educated than most software engineering interns who were still in college. And while it was true that I didn't have a degree in computer science, I was far from a beginner—I'd spent the last three years writing complicated mathematical algorithms.

The solution took me only a few minutes to write. When I sent it in, it took all of my self-control to not call out how weird it was that they'd sent me Project Euler Problem 1, but by then I'd learned to bite my tongue.

I got the job.

Carter called me with the offer: Software Engineer I in the site reliability engineering group. The cash component of the offer was attractive—it was more than I was making at the time, though not by much, and still a little low for the position—but the equity component sounded rather low, much lower than I would be getting anywhere else. I asked for an increase in stock, pointing out that the small equity component of my compensation left me with a lower total compensation than I was willing (or financially able) to accept. Uber came back with a small equity bump of a few shares. I protested again and explained that I wasn't interested in the job or the offer if they refused to give me a competitive equity package. Uber came back again, and this time, they came back not with an increase in pay or equity but with an inflated share price. At this "new" share price they quoted me, which Carter implied was based both on their latest 409A valuation and on a future expected valuation of the company, my total compensation was finally where I needed and wanted it to be.

Before I accepted, I spent more time researching Uber's workplace environment. I still couldn't find anything negative online,* so I went a step further, asking my software engineer friends what they thought. Every one of them had the same answer: Uber was *the* cool place to work, it was the best place to do cutting-edge engineering work, it was the place everyone wanted to be. I spoke to several recruiters who worked at external recruiting firms, each and every one of whom showered Uber with praise. "With Uber on your résumé," one recruiter told me, "you can go anywhere, be anything." I went on several more Uber rides, and again I asked the drivers what they thought about the company. This time I pushed them even harder than I had before, asking them if they knew any other drivers who were having bad experiences. But they were universally positive and said the same thing I'd heard

---

* I didn't know it at the time—and it didn't come up in any of my Google searches about Uber's workplace environment—but there had been some negative press about Uber, including news about the Uber executive Emil Michael threatening the technology journalist Sarah Lacy.

before: fares were down because of intense competition with Lyft, but they were sure Uber would bring them back up; in general, they liked driving for Uber.

Feeling reassured, I put aside my wariness about the Project Euler and equity incidents and accepted the job.

I was one of the first new employees to show up at Uber's headquarters on orientation day, November 30, 2015. I walked into 1455, stopped at one of the lobby desks to obtain a temporary badge, and made my way up in the elevator. When I stepped out on the fourth floor, into its mirrored black elevator bank, I couldn't help thinking that it looked like the Death Star, with its pitch-black walls, ceiling, and floors. At one end of the elevator bank was a lobby area with a marble reception desk, the black Uber logo with its curved, stylized U and R bolted to the wall above it, and a row of couches in the center of the room. As I sat waiting for the other new Uber employees to arrive, I realized this lobby alone was larger than any of the startup offices I'd worked in before.

The rest of the new Uber class slowly trickled in, and the Uber employees running the orientation told us that we were now "nUbers." Everyone was lined up, first to hand in passports and green cards and driver's licenses and then to pose for badge photos, which were taken in front of one of the lobby's many blank white walls. When I stood before the camera, I tried to give an elegant, pretty smile, but I couldn't help myself: I was so excited to be there that I couldn't help but let a goofy, giddy smile light up my face.

We were ushered into a conference room and each given our own MacBook, which was set up with security and tracking software, email, two-factor authentication, and the internal chat application. (By then, I took being handed a brand-new several-thousand-dollar laptop for granted; we all did.) We briefly toured part of the floor—the Death-Star-like, black-walled cafeteria that turned into the all-hands space every Tuesday morning, the bath-rooms, the IT help desk, the rows of desks and conference rooms, and a glimpse at what we were told was "the notorious war room." Then the engineers were whisked out of the building and into a Muni train beneath Market Street. While business and marketing folks stayed at HQ, we were headed to one of Uber's engineering offices down the street.

There were three different training programs that I needed to complete as a new Uber engineer. The first was Engucation, a week filled with daily classes on Uber's engineering culture and prac-tices, distributed systems, on-call routines, security practices, and so much more. One of my Engucation classes was taught by Thuan Pham, Uber's CTO. At the beginning of the week, my fellow new engineers and I had no idea how the Uber application actually worked, and by the end we knew how to write code at Uber.

Before I'd joined the company, I knew that Uber's engineering operation was massive, but I had no idea just how massive the whole mess really was. The Uber phone application was not one code base, like the other "monolithic" applications that I'd worked with; instead, the Uber application was made up of over one thou-sand smaller applications, called microservices, each staffed by a dedicated team of engineers. During my Engucation classes, I tried to wrap my head around what the computing infrastructure underneath all of these applications actually looked like. It was that infrastructure—the servers, the operating systems, the networks, and all of the code that connected the applications together—that I would be working on, that I would need to make better, more reliable, and more fault-tolerant.

After Engucation came more specialized training to prepare new hires for their particular roles within the company. New data scientists spent time with their data science teams, front-end developers learned how to work with the front-end code, and I would embed with one of the site reliability engineering (SRE) teams and learn the basics before I could join my permanent team. Eamon assigned me to one of his SRE teams for this phase of training. It was a ragtag team of two engineers, Clement and Rick, two of the best site reliability engineers in the company, responsible for keeping some of its most critical pieces of software running. Together, they'd assign me small tasks to work through. I loved working with them; Rick with his headphones on, bobbing his head along to whatever new DJ he'd discovered on Sound-Cloud; Clement elbowing him a few times a day and asking him about a problem that they were trying to solve together. By the end of my brief tour with their team, I felt I knew enough about Uber's site reliability engineering practices to receive my permanent assignment: a position on the cloud team.

But before I could start work on the cloud team, I had to complete the last step of the Uber employee onboarding agenda: a three-day-long training program called Uberversity. New employees from all over the world had been flown into San Francisco for

Uberversity after completing Engucation (or the business, marketing, sales equivalent training course) and role-specific training at their home offices. As one of the site reliability engineering managers put it, "Engucation is like high school, where you sort of get a vague idea of what Uber is like; Uberversity is like college, where you finally learn what Uber is *really* all about."

On the first day of Uberversity, hundreds of new employees from every team and country gathered in one of the unmarked Market Street offices. After we found our seats in the large room, the very first thing we were told was that we were not allowed to date "TK." The room buzzed with confusion as everyone began talking to one another. One of the men at my table leaned over and asked the woman next to him, "Who the fuck is TK?" She shrugged and whispered, "I don't know." The woman onstage continued, saying that she knew all of us wanted to date TK, but it was, she said with a sigh, against the rules.

After that strange beginning came classes in business, communications, security, engineering, benefits, and more. In one class, we learned the fourteen Uber values, which we were supposed to embody at all times: "Superpumped," "Always Be Hustlin'," "Let Builders Build," "Meritocracy and Toe-Stepping," "Principled Confrontation," "Big Bold Bets," "Celebrate Cities," "Make Magic," "Inside Out," "Optimistic Leadership," "Be Yourself," "Be an Owner not a Renter," "Champion's Mindset," and "Customer Obsession."

Halfway through Uberversity, there was a competition for "most interesting person." Presented as a team-building exercise, it was led by a high-ranking software engineering director. Each table nominated one person who was the most interesting person at that table, and then all of the nominees walked up to the stage, where he was supposed to choose the winner. After telling the story of my upbringing to my table, I was nominated, and walked up to the stage with the other nominees.

Once we were all lined up onstage, the software engineering director pointed to one of the women at the other end of the stage. "You," he said. "And *you*," he said, pointing to the next woman. "And you," pointing to the other woman. "Aaand, *you*," he said, pointing to me. "All of you," he said, "step down, and go back to your tables." I paused for a moment and laughed out loud, thinking it was a joke. There's no way, I thought to myself, that this guy just eliminated all of the women by accident. I paused for a little too long, and he noticed I was still standing there onstage. He shot me an angry look and beckoned me to return to my table. I stepped down and watched as he then picked the most interesting man.

As part of Uberversity, Uber rented out a bar and held a happy hour each evening for all of the new employees. At the end of the day, I watched as my classmates grabbed their wristbands for the bar, but I turned around and went home. I didn't want to go. I had a bad feeling in the pit of my stomach, though I didn't yet know why.

On the last day of Uberversity, we had an hour-long Q&A with "TK," who, we all finally realized, was Uber's CEO, Travis Kalanick. Afterward, the entire class of new recruits and several members of the Uberversity training staff gathered on the stage for a photo. Nearly everyone in the photo is wearing a black

"Uberversity 2015" T-shirt—everyone, that is, except for some of the older Uberversity staff members, a few people standing in the back, and me.

The Christmas season was quickly approaching. On Friday, December 18, Uber held its annual holiday party. During the weeks leading up to the party, when I was going through the various new employee training programs, the party was all everyone talked about. Over lunch, people were making bets about which famous musician would perform at the party; because there had been a private Beyoncé concert on the infamous "Vegas trip," everyone was sure that she (or someone nearly as famous) would be the evening's musical guest. I'd never been to a Silicon Valley holiday party before; the only Christmas parties I'd ever been to were the ones at my family's church and the loud, drunken physics department parties at Penn. This was going to be totally different. From the way people talked about it, it was *the* event of the year, and Uber was a company that prided itself on lavish, blowout parties. It seemed like everyone around me had been planning what they would wear and whom they would bring for months in advance.

After much consideration and some very careful googling about what women wore to Silicon Valley holiday parties, I bought a purple velvet dress that was neither too conservative nor too revealing. Now all I needed was a date. I was single at the time and had sworn off dating, so I asked Kristin—an old friend from ASU who was now living and working in San Francisco—to go with me.

Uber rented out two gigantic buildings at one of the piers on the Embarcadero for the party. It was raining hard that night, and when we arrived—in an Uber, of course—we ran through the rain into the first building, where we waited in a long line as people checked us in and took our coats.

Inside, everyone was dressed to the nines, laughing and mingling over drinks under dancing, flashing lights. In another room, there was a "silent disco," where everyone wore headphones in which a DJ's music was blaring. Staff members waited at the walkway between the two buildings, where they were handing umbrellas to party guests. Kristin and I grabbed an umbrella and ran to the next building, where we found a regular disco under way, complete with a famous DJ and a dance floor. The first building had been one of the nicest parties I'd ever seen, but this one blew them all away—even the party in the Philadelphia Art Museum I'd attended when I first started at Penn. It was sleek and sophisticated, and it had everything. The other employees didn't seem to think that it was especially fancy, but for me—someone who grew up in poverty, had never gone to prom, and had never gone to a real party aside from the orientation party at Penn—it was like something out of a movie. Kristin and I laughed as we compared it with the old parties we used to frequent at ASU, where fifty of us would cram into someone's two-bedroom apartment with a cheap keg from the drive-through liquor store and dance around the apartment complex pool for hours.

We grabbed some drinks from one of the many open bars, ran to the dance floor, and danced the night away. I didn't know many people at the company yet, and I was glad to have a close friend there with me. At one point, between songs, I hopped off the dance floor to catch my breath. From where I was standing, near the DJ booth, I could see the entire floor of the building, and that's when it hit me: almost everyone at the party was standing off to the side, and only a handful of the guests were dancing. I didn't understand why more people weren't out there, enjoying the party.

As I stood there, surveying the scene, I realized that Travis Kalanick was standing right next to me. I turned to him. "Why isn't anyone dancing?" I yelled over the music, pointing to the sidelines where most of the employees were standing and drinking. He stared out at the dance floor. I joked that it was a waste of a good DJ. "You should go out there," I said, "and encourage everyone to dance." I went back onto the dance floor and danced in my heels until my feet were numb. Kristin and I stayed until the very end, when the lights came back on and people started to dismantle the sound stage.

Though I had enjoyed the party, I couldn't shake the feeling that something was wrong. Between the weird things that had happened at Uberversity and the lack of joy at the party, it seemed like something was very off about this company, though I couldn't figure out exactly what it was. I tried to ignore the alarms going off in my head, because I hadn't even really started working yet. My first day on my new team was Monday, only a few days away, and I hoped, with all of my heart, that I was wrong about Uber.

CHAPTER SEVEN

As I stepped off the BART train and headed up Market Street toward the office that Monday, I was so happy that my walk intermittently broke into a skip. Over the last three weeks, I'd learned how to deploy new code to Uber's servers, how to hunt down bugs in the code, and how to find and fix problems when the software stopped working and the app had an outage. Now I was ready to jump in and do some real work, to fix real problems and write code that would go into the software that powered the Uber app. With Christmas only a few days away, I wanted to dive in and get started before I went back to Arizona to spend the holidays with my family. I couldn't wait to go home and tell my family and friends about my new job at Uber. They were all so proud of me and couldn't believe that their little Susan had graduated from Penn and landed herself a fancy engineering job in Silicon Valley. Many of my friends back home drove for Uber, too, and I wanted to ask them how I could make the app better for drivers.

At the time, Uber was trying to move its computing operations from its own data centers onto cloud providers. The engineers on the cloud SRE team I was joining were not familiar with the particular technology they were using to accomplish this, but I had used it in the past, so they were excited to have me on board. I was excited, too. I knew that moving Uber to the cloud wasn't going to be easy, but I was up for the challenge. It was the complexity of the challenge that attracted me: Uber's software was incredibly complicated, maintained by thousands of engineers who were making changes to it every single day. Moving Uber's computing operations to the cloud would mean we'd have to make the software changes without disrupting the millions of rides that were happening every day. The stakes were extremely high: if we messed up, then people's rides could be lost in the system, or drivers could lose money. It was like renovating a house while people were still living in it: we had to work around them, without disrupting their daily lives. Everything had to be architected out and planned with extreme care.

I didn't yet have a desk with my new team, so when I arrived that morning, I sat at a temporary desk next to Rick, Clement, and the rest of their team, under the bright, colorful Christmas lights some of the other engineers and I had just put up around the desks. Before I started my first big cloud assignment, I had a few things to knock off my to-do list—various SRE onboarding tasks that I'd been given during Engucation, tasks that were intended to familiarize me with Uber's software deployment process. That ate up most of the morning. After lunch, I picked up my laptop and walked around the office, looking for the perfect place to sit and finish my very last onboarding task before diving into my new work for the cloud team. There weren't many people in the office that day, so I had my pick of the couches and window seats. Most people had already begun their Christmas vacations or left the country for Uber-sponsored "workations" in exotic foreign locales. (Uber encouraged employees to spend time working with their coworkers over the holidays rather than with their families and offered employees free all-inclusive trips almost anywhere in the world if they chose work over family. Needless to say, I'd chosen family.) I eventually settled on a cozy little nook near the kitchen, one that looked straight across the open office and had a nice view of the courtyard. I carefully set my coffee cup on the upholstery beside me, sat my computer on my lap, put my feet up, and got to work.

A few minutes later, a notification popped up in the top right corner of my screen. It was a chat message from my new manager, Jake, asking about the status of the onboarding tasks and offering to help me finish them up if I was having any trouble. The particular task I was working on at the time was one that Rick had assigned to me: I was supposed to reimage a server, which meant erasing and reinstalling the operating system and software on a computer. I thanked Jake for his offer and explained that I was working with Rick to get it done and that I would definitely ask him for help if I needed it. Then he changed the conversation.

He started telling me about his upcoming vacation to Hawaii, saying he was "looking to sit back and get into trouble."

"I can't get into too much trouble on the day to day," he added. "Have to think about work."

I looked up from my laptop and stared across the open office in front of me. I had no idea what he was talking about. I tried to think of something to say in response. I'd spoken to him twice before, only briefly—once at a new-hire outing, and a second time when I ran into him at the holiday party. He seemed well liked by the other employees and managers, and I wanted to start off on the right foot with my new supervisor. "True, true," I typed, hoping that would be the right thing to say.

"And vacations," he continued, "have some special rules attached to them in my relationship. It is an open relationship but it's a little more open on vacations haha."

Wait, I thought to myself, *what now?*

I had to reread his message a few times to make sure I was reading it correctly. *He can't seriously be talking to me about his open relationship.* I tried to ignore it and bring the conversation back to the onboarding task I was working on, but he had no intention of letting me change the subject.

"It started out as a case by case basis thing," he said.

My jaw dropped and I nearly threw my hands up in exasperation. *He's really going to keep going, isn't he?*

He kept going.

"When we first started dating 18 months ago I was going out to a party house in Tahoe and this girl I had just been dating was going to be there but my gf wasn't. She said sex was sex and it was no big deal if something happened during that weekend."

Oh, God, I thought. *This guy can't be for real.*

". . . and I returned the favor when she went to Burning Man."

What the hell?

"Honestly, it favors her more than it favors me . . ."

How is this guy my new manager? I thought. I looked up from my laptop and surveyed the floor, hoping to spot a coworker or two, looking for *anyone* I could show these chats to, trying to find someone who could serve as a witness in case Jake continued. But the desks around me were empty.

Shit, I thought, *what do I do?*

". . . she can go and have sex any day of the week . . ."

Oh, God, please stop . . .

". . . it takes a herculean effort for me to do the same . . ."

He wasn't going to stop.

I knew exactly where he was going with this. I put my hands back on the keyboard—Command-Shift-4—and started taking screenshots of the chat messages as they popped up on my screen. It was almost second nature to me by this point and had been since my final year at Penn: take a screenshot, email it to myself, share it with someone else for safekeeping, back it up to several cloud services, print off a hard copy, repeat.

I started to feel sick to my stomach when I realized what was going on. I wanted to believe this wasn't really happening, that it was just a misunderstanding or mistake, so that I could move on and not have to deal with it. But there was no mistaking what this was. Then I felt a wave of relief wash over me when I remembered that I worked at a large company, one with a sizable human re-sources department. Back then, I still believed that HR was there to protect employees, so I was sure that if I reported what had happened, they wouldn't retaliate against me; they would take care of it with a minimal amount of drama so that I could get to work on building up Uber's cloud computing capabilities.

When I got home from work that evening, I looked through all of Uber's internal documentation about reporting issues to HR until I found the representative assigned to our engineering team. I told the HR representative that my new manager had just sent me a string of chat messages about his sex life, one that led to his propositioning me, and that I needed to meet with someone from HR to report what had happened.

I didn't return to the engineering office the next day. Instead, I took Muni to the Uber headquarters, where my meeting with HR was scheduled to take place. When I arrived, I was ushered into the back of the building, where I found myself standing in front of a long row of conference rooms whose windows had been painted over with an opaque coating so that nobody could see what was happening inside. An iPad mounted on the wall next to each room flashed the words "Private Meeting." Every room was occupied.

I stood outside and waited. The desks around me were empty for as far as I could see. I sat down at one of them and imagined what it would be like to work in this fancy and quiet office, imagined myself coding in the silence and working without any noise-canceling headphones, not knowing that I'd be working in that exact spot only a few months later. I was still lost in my daydream when one of the doors opened and a brunette woman in heels walked toward me.

"Susan?" she asked, stretching out her hand toward mine. I nodded. "I'm Karen." We shook hands. "Let's talk in here," she said, beckoning to one of the conference rooms. As we entered the room, she pressed a button on the room's iPad. A new message flashed across the iPad's screen: "Private Meeting."

We sat down across from each other, and she pulled out her computer to take notes. I told her about everything that had happened and showed her the chat messages Jake had sent me on Uber's HipChat app.

"He's my new boss," I said, "and on my very first day on his team he sent me these messages."

I explained that this made me extremely uncomfortable, and she nodded along, a look of concern on her face. Then she shared her thoughts: yes, she said, Jake was definitely propositioning me, which was not just inappropriate but unacceptable and constituted sexual harassment. She assured me that the situation would be taken care of.

"Start your holiday vacation *now*," she urged, "and don't talk to *anyone* about what happened. We'll let you know when you can come back." In the meantime, she assured me, HR would speak with Jake, look over the chat messages, and run a little investigation into the matter; she would get back to me as soon as they'd concluded their investigation.

Following Karen's instructions, I went straight home after our meeting and packed up my things. Before I left for the airport, I emailed the screenshots of Jake's messages to Karen. As I read back over his chat messages, I couldn't shake the feeling that something was off. I kept telling myself that Uber would take care of this, but at the same time it seemed that there was something terribly wrong about it all—about Jake's brazen harassment (*why,* I wondered, *did he feel comfortable propositioning me on my very first day?*), about my meeting with Karen, about the floor of empty desks, about the long row of conference rooms that were each occupied for a "Private Meeting." There was something about the meeting with Karen that reminded me of my meeting with the dean of graduate studies at Penn, in which I was told that everything would be taken care of, that everything would be fixed. I felt sick to my stomach when I remembered how that meeting had turned out, how I'd lost everything.

While I was in Arizona for Christmas, my sense of unease about the situation only grew. My friends and family, who were excited about my fancy new job, had all sorts of questions for me about how I liked working at Uber, and I didn't know what to say. *Should I tell them,* I wondered, *about what really happened, or should I pretend everything is okay? Is everything actually okay?* As I confided in my sisters about the chat messages and my meeting with HR, I found myself growing frustrated. I'd worked so hard and made it through an Ivy League school all the way to a prestigious job at the most valuable startup in Silicon Valley history, only to find that Silicon Valley wasn't much better than the world I'd left behind. I'd worked so hard—for what? To be sexually harassed by my new manager on my first day on his team?

The New Year rolled around, and I returned to the office along with all the other employees who were coming back from family holidays and workations. I hadn't heard anything from HR while I was away, and the issue was still unresolved. I walked back into the office without knowing if I was supposed to be there, without knowing what (if anything) I was supposed to be working on, and it felt strange; I felt like I was doing something wrong. I confided in Eamon, the manager who had recruited me, about what had happened. I begged him not to tell HR that I told him, because I'd promised Karen I wouldn't tell anyone. He was horrified about the situation and apologized for Jake's behavior. I could tell he felt awful about recruiting me and bringing me onto a team where I'd been harassed.

While I waited for the results of HR's investigation, I ran into another unexpected problem. I'd just been given access to an on-line account where I could see the RSUs (restricted stock units) I'd been given as part of my compensation. When I logged in to the system, I was shocked to find that the value of the RSUs was far, far less than Carter had told me. I contacted a member of Uber's equity team, who confirmed that Carter and the recruiting team had significantly inflated the value of the stock; he encouraged me to ask HR and the recruiting team to adjust my number of RSUs so that it matched the amount I'd been promised when I accepted Uber's job offer, which would have meant more than doubling my number of RSUs. HR and the recruiting team, however, refused to follow the equity team's recommendation. Instead, they said that I should realize that the Uber stock would *eventually* be worth what I'd been told. (As of the writing of this book, after Uber's IPO, I can confirm that the stock price has never even come close to reaching the amount I was told. Uber's recruiter told me that it would be worth approximately $183,182.50; it is, at the time of writing, worth $21,500.)

I was dumbfounded. The inflated stock price—which I now

knew had been a lie—was the reason I'd eventually accepted Uber's offer. With the *actual* stock price, my compensation was much lower than I had agreed to. But pushing back against HR didn't get me anywhere. Instead, I was sent to Charles, the director of the site reliability engineering department. Uber had pulled a bait and switch on him, too, he told me: after he joined the company, he had compared the value of his equity with the value they'd promised and was angry when he discovered they'd significantly inflated the value. This wasn't a common tactic in Silicon Valley, he said—most companies gave a fair value estimate of their equity—but he had learned to make his peace with what Uber had done. "It's still worth a lot of money," he said. He urged me to drop it, so I did.

Shortly after that, I was summoned to meet with Karen regarding my sexual harassment complaint. She told me that Uber had concluded its investigation and found that Jake had indeed sexually harassed me. However, she said, Jake was a high performer, and this was his very first offense, so they didn't feel comfortable giving him anything more than a stern talking-to. Then she gave me a "choice": I could stay on the cloud team, with Jake as my manager—though I would likely receive a bad performance review from him because I had turned down his advances and reported him to HR—or I could transfer to a different SRE team.

I couldn't believe what I was hearing. I asked her to repeat herself, but there was no mistake. Uber wasn't really giving me much of a choice, I said. I explained that I wanted to stay on the cloud team, because cloud was my area of expertise and that was what I was hired—and wanted—to work on. Furthermore, I argued, Jake shouldn't be allowed to retaliate against me for turning him down and reporting him to HR. As I was speaking, Karen interrupted me and said that "technically" I wouldn't have a retaliation claim if Jake gave me a bad performance review, because Uber had given me "the option" to avoid retaliation. (As I later learned, this was a lie; retaliating against me in this way would have been illegal.) After repeating that this didn't seem like much of a choice, I opted to transfer to another team. As our meeting came to an end, she told me that this meeting and all details of what had happened were completely confidential, and I wasn't allowed to share them with anyone for any reason. The way she said this last part made it sound as though I would be violating my employment agreement and/or the law by discussing it with anyone (another thing that I later learned wasn't true). At the time, I believed her and was frightened by her warning.

I wasn't allowed to remain on the team where I felt I had the most value to contribute, and to make matters worse, the choice of my new team wasn't up to me. I had a brief respite from the confusion when Eamon was tasked by HR and SRE with managing me until I was moved to a new team. I liked working with Eamon; he was a kind, hardworking, and compassionate manager who tried very hard to make sure that the people who worked with him were happy, fulfilled, and respected. I wanted to keep working with him, but the teams he directly managed didn't have any room for me. I petitioned Charles to let me work with one of the other cloud-related teams but was instead pushed into the newly formed "consulting SRE team."

Out of over a thousand microservices, only the most business-critical ones had site reliability engineers on their engineering teams, and those site reliability engineers made sure that the software was always up and running. The other microservice teams that didn't have site reliability engineers desperately wanted them, but there weren't enough to go around (it was always much easier to hire general software engineers than specialized reliability engineers). The newly formed consulting SRE team, to which I'd just been assigned, was created to solve this problem. It was the engineering SWAT team of the company: whenever there was an important microservice team whose software was unreliable and causing problems in the Uber app, the consulting SRE team would jump in, help the team fix their code, and then move on to the next team who needed help. As a part of this team, I would no longer report directly to Eamon, but to a manager named Duncan.

I was disappointed and frustrated by how the situation had played out. HR had confirmed that I'd been treated inappropriately, but I was the one who was punished for it. I had to choose, in that moment, whether I would fight against HR's decision or try to move on, keep my head down, work hard, and hope that it never happened again. I bitterly remembered my experience at Penn and how I'd escalated the situation as high as I could, only to have my dreams come to an end and my degree torn away from me. If I fought against this decision, I wondered, would Uber do the same thing? Would I be fired, be pushed out, or—even worse—have to find a new career again? I wasn't ready to give up on software engineering, on Silicon Valley, or on Uber—and I felt like I hadn't even given my software engineering career a real chance yet. I decided that I was going to work as hard as I could, learn as much as I could, and hope that I could move on and leave the situation behind.

After being assigned to the consulting team, I was moved away from the other site reliability engineers to an area of the engineering office that was almost completely empty. "You need a break," one of the SRE managers told me when I inquired about my new seat assignment, "and we don't want you to run into anyone from the cloud team." I looked around. There was nobody else, just me, completely alone, for a good twelve rows of desks. I felt a little lonely and missed the fun I used to have sitting next to the other site reliability engineers. To keep from getting depressed about it, I told myself that at least if I was all alone, I could keep my head down and avoid being harassed.

One morning, as I walked to my empty stretch of desks, I noticed someone else sitting only a few desks away: it was one of the engineers from the cloud team. He gave me a big smile, said "hello," then put his headphones on and began working. Over the next several weeks, a handful of other engineers joined him, even though none of them were given official approval to move their desks near mine. "I don't want you to have to sit alone," one of them said before giving me a hug. I didn't tell any of them what had happened; I didn't have to. But it didn't last very long: after half a dozen people—including several of the other engineers on our SRE consulting team—had moved their desks near mine, I was reassigned to a different desk, in a different office, in a building several blocks away. Over the next few months, the game of musical chairs continued. Whenever I fought my desk reassignment and asked to sit with all of the other site reliability engineers, my job was threatened; I'd be told that if I kept fighting it, there would no longer be a place for me at the company. Eventually, I learned to keep quiet and let them move my desk to headquarters, where I found myself surrounded by teams I didn't know. I was all alone again.

Refusing to be completely isolated at Uber, I befriended several other women on the engineering teams, many of whom belonged to a group called LadyEng. The group had been founded the year before I arrived, and most of the women who worked in technical roles were members of LadyEng. The group wasn't very formal— most of our interactions with one another happened in a few chat rooms and over lunches in the cafeterias—but, over time, we all got to know each other.

Whenever we got together, I listened as the other women talked about harassment and discrimination that they were currently facing or had faced in the past. Just like me, they'd all learned the hard way that HR was there to protect the company, not the employees; they all seemed resigned to the fact that Uber's HR department wouldn't do anything about the mistreatment they experienced, and they viewed reporting things to HR as (at best) a formality that would lead nowhere. Many of them even said they'd given up on reporting things, because they knew from experience that HR would retaliate against them. Some of their stories sounded pretty similar to my own—something that I didn't think very much of until one of the women mentioned that the manager who had mistreated her was also named Jake. The pieces all fell into place for the first time, and we realized that several of us had experienced harassment or similarly discriminatory treatment from the same manager and, furthermore, that HR had given us identical spiels each time one of us reported him: "this," they told each of us, "is his first offense." Just like me, the other women had believed HR when they were told it was Jake's "first offense."

One night, when I went out for drinks with several other women in the site reliability engineering department, we swapped stories.

"Oh, Jake," one of my coworkers said with a bitter laugh as she looked into her drink, "he pulled that shit on me, too. 'I'm in an open relationship,' he said."

We all groaned.

"Gross," I said. "I can't believe he said that to you, too."

"You know what I said?" she asked as she burst into laughter. "I said, 'Well, guess what, man? So is half of San Francisco. You're not special!'"

With us at the bar was a young engineer named Laura, who was working in our group as an intern. When she started her internship, she was put on the chaos testing team, responsible for one of the most difficult, messy systems that Uber was running. Anyone else would have failed, and failed hard, at that job, but not Laura—she was too determined, too tough to give up. By the end of her internship, she had earned the respect of every single engineer in our department. Uber had offered her a job, and that night she was trying to decide whether she would accept. All of us at the table had been encouraging her to join. She had become a core part of our group, and, to be honest, I don't think any of us thought we could survive without her. But I felt awful sitting there with Laura and the other women, encouraging her to work with us even as we all shared stories about being sexually harassed. I felt like a coward and a hypocrite. I couldn't bear the thought of Laura being harassed. I wasn't going to let it happen, and I was determined to do something about it.

"You should be in the world, but not of the world," my father used to tell me. Even now, I can hear him saying it, with his crooked smile, in his gentle, confident voice. That's what he tried to do, throughout his life: to live *in* the world, flawed as it was, while at the same time holding himself to a higher standard. It wasn't enough for him to work hard, to go to college, to provide for his family. No, he had to have a good heart, to always try to do the right thing regardless of the consequences, and to each day try to be a better man than he had been the day before. On one cold desert evening, when we were walking through the neighborhood, he told me that it wasn't easy to walk this line, that it wasn't easy to be good. It was much easier, he explained, to be like everyone else. It was much easier, he said, to do nothing.

I didn't want to be the person who did nothing, but I wasn't sure what—if anything—I *could* do. After racking my brain for answers, and talking to several of the other LadyEng members about what had happened to me and to other women in the company, I still didn't have any clue. So I decided to just take it one step at a time. I couldn't fix HR, I couldn't change the company's culture by myself, and I couldn't file complaints on behalf of all the other women who had been harassed or push HR about their cases, but I *could* go and ask for my own case to be reopened; I *could* put up a bigger fight. It was obvious that HR had messed up—in my case and in the past—but if I could convince engineering leadership that the investigation had been conducted poorly, maybe HR would do a better job in the future.

I decided to escalate my situation, and met with Charles again. To my surprise, he already knew about what had happened with Jake, and he even seemed to know about Jake's past offenses (though, just like Karen, he insisted that Jake's propositioning me was "his first offense"). I asked him why Jake hadn't been punished, and he repeated the same things that Karen had said to me earlier: Jake was a high performer, this was his first offense, and it wouldn't be fair, he said, to punish him and potentially ruin his career for something that was just "an innocent mistake." He then parroted the same "retaliation" lines I'd heard from Karen: pulling me off Jake's team wasn't retaliation, because I'd been "given an option," and I chose to leave. As we sat there in one of the large conference rooms, shielded by the opaque glass, he gave me a stern look and asked me what I wanted out of this.

I paused for a moment, confused, wondering what he meant. "What do I *want*?" I asked, hoping he would clarify.

"Yes," he said quietly, "what are you trying to get out of this?"

I took a deep breath. Then I told him that I didn't want to be retaliated against; that I wanted to be on the cloud team, working on the things that I was good at, using my skills to benefit Uber and Uber's engineering team; that I wanted to do my work without being harassed. He shook his head and told me that he couldn't put me back on the cloud team, because I'd receive a bad performance review for reporting Jake to HR and for turning down his advances. "You don't want a bad review, do you?" he asked.

I felt like I was talking to a broken record. Regardless of what I said, he just repeated Karen's words back to me, over and over. As I walked out of the conference room and back to my desk, it was clear to me that Charles wasn't going to do anything to help me or prevent the same thing from happening to others.

As demoralizing as the situation was, I was happy enough in my personal life that I didn't let it bring me down: I was living in the big Berkeley house, spending all of my free time learning and studying and playing the violin, having fun exploring San Francisco with my friends, and best of all I was falling in love.

Shortly after I'd moved to the Bay Area, Chad Rigetti and I connected on Facebook. Chad, the founder of Rigetti Quantum Computing, popped up as a "suggested friend" shortly after our interview, and it was then that I saw his face for the very first time. I couldn't believe *that* was the guy I'd spoken to on the phone during my job search back at Penn. With his blond hair, chiseled jaw, broad shoulders, and hazel eyes, he was the most gorgeous man I'd ever seen. I later described him to my friends (who thought I was out of my mind) as a cross between Michael Fassbender and Albert Einstein, "but," I would add, with a silly grin, "he is hotter than Fassbender and more brilliant than Einstein."

I added him as a friend, and to my complete surprise he accepted. Over the next few months, as our Facebook friendship evolved into liking each other's pictures and updates, I developed the biggest schoolgirl-style crush on him. My heart would pound in my chest every time he posted a new photo or an update about his company, and I daydreamed about our going out together and talking about physics and philosophy over dinner and drinks. I was certain, however, that these would never be more than daydreams. After I moved to California, Chad reached out and asked me if I'd like to meet him and his team at the company's new office in Berkeley. I'd never forgotten our phone interview, and I was excited to meet him, but I didn't want to bring the ambiguity of a crush into a professional interaction, so I declined.

Every Christmas, I send out hundreds of Christmas cards to friends, family, and colleagues. To break the ice with Chad, I decided to ask him for his address so I could add him to my Christmas card list. Then, one weekend in January, he asked me to meet him for brunch. This time, it wasn't lunch with the team, or coffee at the office—it was *brunch*. I arrived at the little Berkeley café a bit early, and waited nervously for him to arrive. I know some people don't believe in love at first sight, but the moment that he walked through the door, I knew he was the love of my life, that we were meant to be together. We spent the rest of the morning getting to know each other, talking about our favorite things, and sharing our plans and dreams for the future. He told me about his love for country music and showed me a video of Garth Brooks, his favorite musician, singing "The River"; I told him about my obsession with the ancient philosophers and about a book I was reading about the Presocratics (the very first philosophers in history, who lived before the time of Socrates).

From the very start, I tried to make it clear to him that I was no longer interested in a job at his company, that I was happy at Uber, and that I wanted (at the very least) to be friends. In my mind, I was thinking, *I don't want a job, I want you.* As we left the café and walked down the street, he reached for my arm, smiled, and said, "Let's take over the world together."

From that moment on, we were inseparable.

In those early months of 2016, I tried to make the best of my situation at Uber and kept my head down, focusing on my day-to-day work. But that proved impossible when, toward the end of March, I heard from one of my colleagues that Jake was telling other people in the site reliability engineering department that I had reported him to HR and that I couldn't "handle" a man like him. Around the same time, I heard that Jake tried to persuade his team to go to a nearby strip club for lunch, which irked not only his team but all the other engineers who overheard him talking about it. Several people reported him to HR and even escalated the complaint to Thuan Pham, Uber's CTO. Again, nothing was done, and, once again, the individuals who reported it were told it was his first offense.

At this point, many people were upset that Uber was turning a blind eye to complaints, and that HR was covering up inappropriate behavior. Ashley, one of my coworkers and a fellow member of LadyEng, bravely escalated the complaints up the SRE and engineering management chain, to Charles, and then to David, Charles's manager. When no disciplinary actions were taken, she and a manager from our department had a meeting with Thuan Pham and asked him why HR and the SRE managers were sweeping complaints under the rug.

Once we all realized that even the CTO wasn't going to do anything about it, we were furious. Many of us had made complaints about Jake's behavior over the past year, and these complaints had gone all the way to Uber's executives, yet the company was acting as if none of these complaints existed. Meanwhile, his behavior was disrupting people's work—a fact that made the situation seem even more absurd.

I got together with several other employees—men and women who either had complained to HR about Jake in the past or who wanted to file new complaints about his behavior—and we decided we would go to HR together. We wanted to all be in the room with an HR representative at the same time so that we could hold Uber accountable, but HR refused to meet with us as a group, citing confidentiality and privacy reasons. Undeterred, we gathered a paper trail and scheduled successive meetings with the HR department so that they couldn't lie to us and tell us there was only one complaint about Jake.

I had the final meeting of the week. As with my last meeting with HR, we met in one of the conference rooms at Uber's

headquarters, the iPad on the door flashing the old familiar message: "Private Meeting." I was the first to arrive, so I took a seat at
the large conference table. Just as I was starting to wonder whether
someone from HR would actually show up, a brunette woman
walked in the door and introduced herself as Jessica. She explained
that she was part of a newly formed "harassment task force" at
Uber and that she'd been assigned to several cases, including this
one. As we sat across from each other at the conference table, I
recounted what had happened with Jake on my first day of work,
my meeting with Karen, the "choice" I'd been given to change
teams or accept a poor performance review, and Charles's inaction
when I escalated the complaint.

She nodded sympathetically while I was speaking, but when I
finished describing the situation to her, she told me that she didn't
understand why I was there.

"We thought you were happy with how the issue was resolved,"
she said, a look of dismay on her face.

"I'm obviously not," I said. "When I reported the chat messages,
Karen told me it was Jake's first offense, but that wasn't true."

"It *was* his first offense," she insisted.

"No," I said, shaking my head, "it wasn't. And you've just had a
series of meetings with people who reported other instances of
sexism and bullying from the same manager."

She sighed. Then, after a long pause, she repeated the same set
of talking points that it seemed like every HR representative had
memorized: when Jake harassed me, it was his first offense; because
it was his first offense, they wouldn't feel comfortable punishing
him; and, furthermore, I couldn't "claim retaliation," because "we

gave you an option" to leave his team. But then she said something I hadn't heard before, something that shook me to my core: "Actually," she said, raising her eyebrows, "all of the other employees were here to talk about *you*."

I felt panicked, afraid, and embarrassed. I felt my face grow hot and knew it had turned bright red. *Could this really be true?* I wondered. *Did everyone else in that group lie to me and then complain about me to HR instead? Is this all in my head?* I endured the rest of the meeting in a daze, walked outside, bought a pack of cigarettes, and sat on the curb outside the building, my head in my hands and tears running down my face.

I felt so ashamed. I couldn't help but wonder whether, in my efforts to get justice for myself and change things at Uber, I'd gone too far. I had so many regrets about what happened at Penn, and I knew that I was frustrated about how Uber had handled the situation with Jake—had I let my regret and frustration cloud my judgment? Had I blinded myself to reality? I racked my brain for any warning signs I might have missed, red flags about my own judgment and discernment I might have ignored. As I sat there, trying desperately to figure out what I'd done wrong, my phone began to buzz; several of my friends and colleagues were asking how my meeting with HR had gone. When I told them about my meeting, and about what Jessica had told me—that this was Jake's first offense; that nobody else had complained about Jake; that everyone else had been there to complain about me instead—they said she'd done the same thing to them, too.

From then on, we gave up all hope of HR ever taking action against Jake or any other manager or employee guilty of bullying, discrimination, or harassment. Our group slowly fell apart, and we stopped talking to each other about what was happening. Talking about it was too demoralizing; it made us feel trapped, angry, frightened. Many of my friends and colleagues vowed to never report anything to HR again. I decided that if anything else happened, I would still document it and report it to HR, even though I knew they wouldn't act on it (if anything, I only expected that reporting things would bring further retaliation). And whenever other employees came to me and asked me for advice, I encouraged them to do the same, because I knew, from my conversations with lawyers during the incident at Penn, how important it was to document and report everything. I knew if there was ever a lawsuit, there would need to be documentation of the complaints, and proof that the company hadn't acted on problems after they'd been reported. After all, whenever harassment, discrimination, or retaliation happened in the workplace, it was the *company*—not the individual who was guilty of the harassment, discrimination, or retaliation—that was legally responsible; in order to hold the company legally accountable for mistreatment, you had to make sure the company knew about the mistreatment and had been given a chance to fix it.

It didn't take long for Uber to retaliate against the people who had either reported Jake to HR in the past or had been part of our group who had met with Jessica from HR. Eamon, who had reported Jake and pushed back against HR, Charles, David, and the executives when no disciplinary action was taken, was forced to leave the company. The official message was that he was "leaving to spend time with his family," but we all knew why he'd been pushed out. Another employee was fired a couple of months later; a few days before he was fired, he told me he'd been warned that he wasn't a "team player." One of the women from our group was threatened and bullied until she was so exhausted that she had to go on medical leave for the next three months.

I was moved once again, to yet another solitary desk away from all of the other site reliability engineers, presumably at the behest of Eamon's replacement and my new skip-level manager (my manager's manager), a large, loud man named Kevin who had worked at Google with Charles and David for many years. Shortly after he started, he told one of my friends that there weren't many women in site reliability engineering because no women were really, truly interested in it.

CHAPTER EIGHT

I didn't know what to do. It was clear to me that Uber was a toxic place to work, but I'd only been at the company for a few months now, and even though leaving was all I could think about, I couldn't do it—not after how quickly I'd left Plaid and PubNub. My only option seemed to be to try my best to survive—to draw the least attention possible to myself, to work hard enough that my contributions could not be denied, and to hope that things would get better.

After working on the SRE consulting team for several months, I noticed that all the different engineering teams I'd been helping fix their software suffered from similar problems. I made a checklist of these common problems—significant problems that caused the microservices to break, which would bring the Uber app down or make it unbearably slow—and wrote down the ways we could fix them. From that point on, whenever I met with a new team, I sat down with them, looked through their code, evaluated the architecture of their microservices, and then together we'd go through the items on my checklist one by one. By the end of the meeting, we had a pretty good idea of what was broken and a clear, step-by-step plan for how to fix it.

The process was working so well that I wondered if we could make a checklist for the whole company to follow. If we could, then the teams wouldn't need a SWAT team to come in and fix everything; instead, they'd be able to fix their own problems. If we could pull this off, it would make a huge difference: the teams that ran the microservices didn't always know that the issues they were facing were problems that other teams had solved before.

Furthermore, there was no standardization across the company for how our software systems should be built. Over a thousand independent microservices, spread out across countless engineering teams, all had to work together for the Uber app to function correctly; these microservices didn't always work together the way they needed to, and the lack of standardization was largely to blame. Whenever these systems failed because they didn't meet basic standards of building reliable software, it meant that riders were abandoned, drivers weren't paid, and destinations were lost mid-trip. This wasn't just an academic exercise in optimization; there were very real consequences for these failures, and I was excited at the prospect of improving the experiences of our riders and drivers.

With my checklist in hand, I realized that if we made a list of architecture standards that made sense for every team and every software system, we could make all the interconnected systems work better and be more reliable. But that wouldn't be enough—teams would still have to be held accountable for meeting those standards. I wondered whether we could come up with a system to certify that microservices were "production-ready" (i.e., ready to go online and be part of the Uber app) if they met a certain threshold—say, if they met 90 percent or higher of the standards on my checklist.

Several engineers in various teams across the company had typed up lists of standards that they used for their own team. Rick—who was undeniably one of the best engineers at the company—had been the first engineer to make a comprehensive list of production-readiness standards that all of the teams he worked with should implement for their microservices. Another site reliability engineer named Paul had also made a list of production-readiness standards, and had even partially automated them. With their help, and with the help of my consulting SRE team colleagues, I went back to the drawing board and looked at the standards that Rick and others had created, my little checklist and the thresholds I had calculated, and the biggest problems our microservices were facing, and I started to dream up a combination of these things—something we could implement to standardize all of Uber's software.

I used my position in the consulting team to trial the new standards system with a handful of teams, and—after quite a bit of trial and error to find the right combination—was happy to see that the new standards were a great success. I then partnered with several other teams who pushed for broad internal adoption, and Roxana, one of the newest women in the SRE department, brilliantly automated the entire standardization system. She worked closely with hundreds of software teams to make sure that the system worked for them, and made it easy and fun for engineers to bring their software up to Uber's new standards.

Uber periodically gave awards to engineers who exemplified its cultural values, handing out one award for each of the fourteen values. Receiving one of these awards was a pretty big deal inside the company. It meant not only that you'd be recognized for your work (something that rarely happened in a company that employed thousands of engineers) but that you would likely receive a promotion and/or a large bonus in your next performance review.

Roxana's work on the automated standardization system was extraordinary, and was directly improving the reliability of all of Uber's software, so I nominated her for one of the awards. When the awards were announced a few weeks later, I checked the list, eager to see Roxana's name. Instead, someone else was given the award. The man who received it was someone I'd worked with in the past, and I couldn't believe he had gotten it over Roxana; his work didn't even come close to having the impact that Roxana's did. It didn't make any sense.

Confused, I contacted the awards committee. But before I did, I went back through the list of previous recipients and noticed that only a few women had ever received one of these awards. I also spoke to other women in the company, and we did an informal tally of the number of times we'd nominated other women for awards. From our calculations, it appeared that women had been nominated with almost the same frequency as men, yet had received far fewer awards. In response, the software engineering director who ran the awards committee said that women weren't winning because women didn't know how to write nominations. There was something familiar about the dismissive way he explained this, so I searched for his name in the company directory. I laughed out loud when I saw his picture in the system and realized he was the same software engineering director who'd made all of the women leave the stage during the "most interesting person" game at my Uberversity.

When I—along with several other women from LadyEng—pushed back, he suggested that a separate award be created for women so that women could receive awards at Uber. I fought hard against this ridiculous proposal until it was off the table. Going forward, I helped other women write nominations for their co-workers, making sure that multiple people read the submissions so that the engineering director who gave out the awards couldn't claim that the nominations were poorly written. Eventually, Roxana and several of the other women were finally given awards for what they'd achieved.

Around the same time, I became what was known as a "bar raiser" at Uber. The title was derived from the idea that every new hire should "raise the bar" at the company, but some of us joked that we were there to raise the bar for how interviews were conducted. At Uber, bar raisers acted as an objective third party in every interview; they were present to make sure that there was no gender, racial, or other discrimination at play in the hiring process and that candidates met Uber's cultural values and standards. In addition, bar raisers were the only people in the interview process who had the authority to veto a hire, even if everyone else interviewing the candidate wanted to hire him or her. I took the job very seriously, attending around three interviews each week and ensuring they were conducted fairly.

Bar raising wasn't easy, but it was well worth the time. I rotated through the company, rarely interviewing candidates for the same teams. Each interview was like being dropped into a completely new company—one where I knew nobody else—and I'd have to listen carefully to each interviewer's recap of an interview as I audited the process. Before each interview, I'd sit down and make a mental list of the things I needed to watch for: make sure the interviewers aren't discriminating against candidates for sex, national origin, sexual orientation, and more; make sure they don't dismiss candidates because they have a foreign accent; make sure they don't ask about family or children, which managers would sometimes refer to as "other obligations outside work."

I soon learned that my efforts were not welcome. Kevin, my skip-level manager, hated that I was a bar raiser. He and my immediate manager, Duncan, told me over and over again that they hated the program and they hated that I was involved in it. I fought to stay involved because I truly felt that I was doing something important to make Uber a better place, but it was no use. Eventually, Kevin and Duncan made it clear that I would be fired if I continued to participate in the program and that I needed to make up a reason why I was leaving the program so that it would not come back on them. "Just say you're too busy," Duncan said with a shrug.

I ended my involvement to keep my job, but I wasn't happy about it.

I was proud of the work I was doing on the consulting team. As teams began to re-architect and debug their code to conform to the new company-wide production-readiness standards, we watched as the downtimes of their microservices hit all-new lows. Wondering if I could make the standardization process general enough that other companies could use it, I obtained permission from Uber's legal department and my managers to share my work with other companies in Silicon Valley. When they, too, found great success from using it, I got a contract with O'Reilly Media—the top publisher of software engineering books—to turn it into a book.

I was thrilled. I couldn't believe I had a book deal, that I was about to fulfill my lifelong dream of becoming a writer. I worked in the Uber offices all day long, then headed back to the big orange house in Berkeley, where I wrote until the early hours of the morning. After learning that I qualified for a special graduate program in computer science at Stanford through a partnership that Uber had with the university for employees with high performance scores, I enrolled and started taking my first real software engineering class. In addition to my Stanford coursework, I kept up my own independent studying. When I wasn't working or writing, I was learning about operating systems, networking, category theory, and new programming languages like Lisp and Go. Even though things were getting worse at work, I tried to ignore the bad parts of Uber and focus on the good things in my life.

What little free time I had, I spent with Chad. We took long walks through Tilden Park, went kayaking on the Russian River, went to Oakland A's baseball games, and shared the details of our weeks with each other. Over the past few months, we'd fallen madly in love. He was busy, too: His startup was growing quickly, and he'd just raised the company's Series A—its first major round of venture capital investment. He worked twelve to fourteen hours every day, from before the sun came up until after dark. I'd never met anyone so wholly devoted to his work: he loved every single thing he did, loved his employees, and loved what they were building together.

The way he felt about his job, and the culture he was cultivating at his company, stood in stark contrast to how I felt about mine. Rigetti Quantum Computing and Uber Technologies were at opposite ends of the spectrum: Chad wanted Rigetti Quantum Computing to be a company filled with joy, where people came into work excited and passionate about the technical challenges of building quantum computers and working as a team to solve hard problems; Uber, on the other hand, was a company driven by aggression, hell-bent on destroying the competition no matter the cost, where it felt like people came into work to tear down, not to build up.

Uber's success was due, in large part, to its aggressive disregard for the law; Travis Kalanick and his team were operating in cities across the world without permission, unashamedly breaking and disregarding laws and regulations—all in the name of "hustle" and "disruption." Unfortunately, as I experienced firsthand that spring and summer, the aggression that had precipitated Uber's meteoric rise was also directed at the lowest-ranking employees in the company. Disregarding laws, rules, and regulations was so entrenched in Uber's culture that managers within the company seemed to believe that various rules—including employment law and basic human decency—no longer applied to them. Berating employees, insulting them, mocking them, and threatening them were all commonplace behaviors that went unpunished. Promotions, bonuses, and praise were often used to manipulate employees, HR, and other managers; after one of my female colleagues received a promotion, she confided in me that she was sure she'd been promoted because her manager had just been reprimanded for sexual harassment and was "trying to cover his ass."

The power dynamics within the company seemed sociopathic. All the managers were vying for their managers' roles, and their managers were trying to get *their* managers' jobs. Nothing was off-limits in these petty power games: projects were sabotaged, rumors were spread, employees were used as pawns. There was no effort to hide these power struggles from low-level engineers like me; to the contrary, our managers told us about them, and we were the ones who ultimately paid the price. These political games had significant consequences: projects were abandoned without notice, wasting thousands of hours of hard work; our company goals and projects were changed so frequently that we rarely knew what we were supposed to be working on; teams were constantly being dissolved and engineers moved from one department to another. We often joked among ourselves that it was a miracle the app even worked at all. The company was in complete chaos.

Managers often dismissed problems with the company's culture as normal startup behavior; but what was happening at Uber was so far beyond anything that would be considered even remotely acceptable at other companies in Silicon Valley. I would share details of what was going on with Chad, my friends, and my family; while they believed me, they often said that it was so far from acceptable or normal workplace behavior that it almost defied belief. In normal, functioning companies, when bad things happened, there were checks and balances to keep individual instances from becoming systemic problems. At Uber, no such checks and balances seemed to exist. Whenever something bad happened—like sexual harassment, verbal abuse, or another form of bullying—instead of the problem being addressed and fixed, it was covered up. Left to seethe and rot, the toxic behavior slowly infected the rest of the company. It was like a disease, one that gradually distorted the moral compasses of employees and managers, who, when they looked at the people around them, only ever saw their own twisted view of the world reflected back at them, reinforcing their awful behavior.

It was generally understood that the entire mess came from the very top; it seemed that Travis Kalanick and Thuan Pham liked watching their employees fight against each other. Anytime I'd meet with my skip-level manager, Kevin, he'd tell me that Charles—his boss—was on his way out and that Kevin had been assured by Charles's boss, David, that the job would soon be his. Then, whenever I'd meet with Charles, I'd learn from him that apparently David was on his way out and Charles would soon take his place. I wasn't the only one they told; almost every one of my friends within the company had heard the same things from them. And I'll never forget a meeting that my team had with David shortly after Uber announced that the company would be pulling out of China later that summer. In the meeting, David told us that, one day, Travis had invited him to his house, where Travis told him all about the China exit; before David left, Travis asked him to keep the China news a secret from Thuan. David then boasted to the twenty or so people in the room that he'd kept the secret from Thuan and he was now sure that Travis would make him the company's CTO.

Beyond the discrimination, mistreatment, and power struggles, the pace of work was intense and relentless. Earlier in the spring, when Arianna Huffington joined the board, Uber had bought so many copies of her new book about the importance of sleep that the offices were filled with huge piles of them. There were stacks of *The Sleep Revolution: Transforming Your Life, One Night at a Time* on every table, in every kitchen, on every empty desk. I remember going into the office kitchen one morning to grab a banana for breakfast, and having to push around stacks of her book that were blocking the food and coffee. It seemed like a sick joke to many of us that Uber was promoting a book that preached the importance of working less, taking naps, and sleeping more, while most of its employees were working over twelve hours every day and many drivers were working hazardously long shifts in order to receive bonuses.

Throughout the spring and summer, there were frequent anti-Uber protests outside the headquarters. Dozens, sometimes hundreds, of people would line up on the sidewalk, and police would patrol the entrance, making sure none of the demonstrators entered the building. While some of the executives used a side door to escape the protests, the low-level employees always had to leave through the front door and walk past the protesters, with whom I had several troubling encounters. Once, a protester followed me from the building to the BART station, where he spit on me. Another time, a group of young men followed me with their phone cameras on, yelling, "You're going viral, bitch!" while asking me if I thought Uber was exploiting drivers. Protesters weren't the only ones who followed me: in the late summer, I was followed home by an aggressive reporter who asked me what I knew about Uber pulling its operations out of China.

Earlier in the year, someone had leaked information to Buzz-Feed about rapes and other sexual assaults that had happened in Ubers. In response, Uber sent a private investigator to the home of a former Uber customer service representative named Morgan Richardson, whom they believed to be the source of the leak. The private investigator harassed Ms. Richardson, and even illegally entered her home. When she reported this to the press and to the police, Uber confirmed that they had hired the investigator and defended his actions, claiming they had "an obligation to look into situations like this." Most employees seemed to shrug it off, as they did every time there was negative press. I heard some of my coworkers say that it was all lies, that rumors were being spread because the press was hell-bent on destroying Uber. But most employees, like me and my friends, kept their mouths shut—we rarely said anything about the company that might be construed as negative, because we were certain that our internal communications were being monitored.

It was in this atmosphere of competitiveness, aggression, and paranoia that, in the summer, Kevin moved me to a position where I was, once again, the only site reliability engineer, and where I had to support over thirty software engineering teams. This meant that if there was an issue with the code, I was responsible for fixing it immediately, no matter the hour of the day or night. With these new demands, my life started to fall apart. I had to put aside the work on my book, had to stop taking violin lessons, and didn't have enough energy to study or learn anymore. It was just like those days back at Plaid, when every moment of my waking life had been focused on endless, relentless engineering grunt work. I was barely sleeping, and would often work long into the night; some nights, I didn't sleep at all. To make matters worse, several of the teams that I was working with were staffed with managers and engineers who were borderline abusive. If I didn't fix something right away because I was helping another team, they would yell at me, threatening to report me to Kevin for "not doing your job." Sometimes, Kevin would defend me in front of the abusive managers, but then he'd start berating me himself, for no reason, a few days later.

The abuse that I endured from my managers grew worse with every passing day. I dreaded going into work, knowing that I'd be yelled at in meetings, that I'd be told I wasn't "doing my job," that I wasn't "working hard enough," even though I was doing everything that my managers asked of me. I wasn't the only one who felt this way. When I told my friends in the other site reliability engineering teams what was going on, they said they had the same problems with their managers and teams, too. Almost every single one of them had started seeing a therapist for anxiety or depression related to the culture of work at Uber; the engineers who'd been at Uber the longest all seemed to have suicidal thoughts. This scared me, because I was starting to develop anxiety and PTSD from my work, too, and I didn't want my mental health to get worse.

As time wore on, and the situation at work grew more and more unbearable, the anxiety and stress from Uber leached into my personal life and threatened to destroy my most important relationships. One day, I got into a nasty argument with Chad. We were arguing about something that wasn't even important, but I felt so defensive and attacked that, afterward, my heart was pounding. I realized that I'd been expecting to be yelled at, just as I always did at work. Everyone I worked with was aggressive, and I was often yelled at or threatened or insulted. But Chad wasn't aggressive, he never once insulted me, and he would never, ever yell at me. In the moment, I couldn't understand why I felt the way I did. I shrugged it off.

Later that same day, I got in another fight, this time with my mother. Again, it stemmed from a disagreement over something relatively minor, and again my heart was pounding. I kept closing my eyes and clenching my jaw, expecting her to yell at me. I realized I was having a panic attack; there was a stabbing pain in my chest, I couldn't take a deep breath, and my blood pressure was so high that I could barely even see the room around me. I was so anxious about being reprimanded that I was completely shutting down. Once I calmed down, I sat thinking about what had happened. It didn't make sense: my mother and I argued from time to time, but my reaction had been totally out of proportion to the seriousness of what we were discussing.

And then it hit me. I was so used to being reprimanded in my meetings at work that I was turning into a terrified, defensive, panicked person. At Uber, disagreeing with management about *anything* elicited a reprimand in one way or another, and so I'd learned to anticipate their reactions and would have a panic attack whenever I realized I needed to disagree with them. Agreeing with them about something would almost always lead to being reprimanded, too: they'd tell me to do something, I'd do it, and then they'd reprimand me for doing it. I tried to defend myself, but it was rarely any use. When they insulted me, I tried to explain to them why I thought that their insult was wrong; whenever they berated me or told me I wasn't doing my job, I listed off the things that I was doing well, trying to explain that I was actually quite good at my job. Nothing I said or did seemed to change their minds.

I was a shy, introverted person, and I hated confrontation. In order to survive in Uber's aggressive culture, I had to shut off the sensitive side of myself and be far more aggressive (and defensive) than I felt comfortable with. I worried that by shutting off the kind, sensitive, quiet, calm parts of myself, I was becoming like the people I disliked—the kind of person who yelled in meetings and who argued at work all day long. I didn't like who I was becoming, didn't feel proud of the tired, bitter, angry young woman whose face I saw in the mirror every morning. My intrinsic nature was joyful, happy, enthusiastic, passionate; *that* was who I was, *that* was who I wanted and needed to be, but I didn't know how to find myself. I felt lost, alone, and terribly afraid.

The situation on my team kept getting worse. Duncan continued to berate me in meetings, saying that I was a bad engineer but that he knew I had it in me to be better. Then I'd meet with Kevin, who would tell me the same thing, adding that he knew I could be a decent engineer if I put some effort into it, because he refused to believe that Ivy League schools gave diplomas to stupid people. Eventually, I stopped fighting back, because I had nothing left in me. I no longer disagreed with them, no longer tried to defend myself when they insulted me. Instead, I just took the abuse, then headed straight to the bathroom after each meeting, where I stood inside one of the empty stalls and cried.

I knew that the only way I could survive at Uber was to transfer to another team. There were a few teams at the company that were rumored to be different, where the engineers were happy and fulfilled and loved their jobs and their managers, and I wanted desperately to join one of them. Because I had perfect performance reviews, had never missed a deadline or left a task unfinished, had a good reputation, and had done good work, I was confident I'd be able to find a team that wanted me. I was overjoyed to find that I had a handful of amazing teams to choose from, with managers who thought I was a good engineer and wanted me to work with them. When I decided on a team—one of the newer cloud teams, where I could finally work on the thing I'd been hired to do—the transfer was approved by HR and by the manager of that team. The only step remaining was for Kevin to approve the move. To my great surprise, he blocked it.

In our next meeting, I confronted him.

"Why did you block my transfer?" I asked, dumbfounded. "Given my performance score, I have every right to transfer. It's company policy. You can't block it. It's not right."

He shook his head, his face turning red. "As your manager, I can block your transfer to another team at any time."

"But why?" I asked. "There's no reason for you to block the transfer. The other manager desperately wants me on his team, and the transfer has already been approved by everyone else. I have a perfect performance review, I've never missed a deadline, I've completed all of my OKRs. All you have to do is say I can go."

"I'm not transferring a performance problem!" he yelled.

"What performance problem?" I asked, confused. "Is it something about my work? Is it something else that I'm not doing right at the office?"

He didn't answer my questions. Instead, he started talking about the difference between project managers and engineers and how there were some people in the SRE department who thought they were "real engineers" because they had the "engineer" title.

"You have what I like to call an 'undocumented performance problem,'" he said. "You're just not technical enough. You don't choose technical work. You're not a real engineer; you're a project manager."

"But *you're* the one assigning me the work," I replied. "If you want me to do something different, why don't you give me different things to do?"

I urged him to look at the additional projects I had accomplished in my spare time: I'd designed new system architectures for teams; I'd compiled the software architecture standards being used *by the entire company.*

He threw his hands up in exasperation.

"Performance problems," he said, "aren't always something that has to do with *work*, but can sometimes be about things *outside of work* or your personal life. Some people have things *about them* that are performance problems. These aren't things about their work, or the kind of work they do, but *who they are.*"

At that moment, I knew exactly what he meant. I'd heard from other SREs who worked with him that he didn't believe women could be *real* SREs, simply because they were women, and now he was basically saying it to my face.

I escalated the situation all the way up the management chain, reminding each and every person that it was company policy that they had to let an employee transfer if he or she was above a certain performance score threshold. But when I brought the issue to Charles, he said that he'd worked with Kevin for years at Google and he trusted his judgment. When I took it to Charles's boss, David, he said the same thing: they'd all worked together at Google, and they trusted each other's judgment. If Kevin thought I had a performance problem, even if there was no documentation or proof of it, then I *was* the performance problem.

As the summer dragged on, things only got worse. Verbal abuse was now a common occurrence in meetings. "How did you get hired?" Kevin once asked me, remarking that he guessed Uber used to have lower hiring standards. "You're not a very good engineer," someone else would say. "You're not an engineer at all." And then there was my favorite: "I know there's an engineer in there somewhere, if you can find her."

I tried to shut out the things Kevin, Duncan, and other managers said to me, and focus on the good things in my life: my relationship, my book, my education, and the actual work I was doing, which was going well. But I couldn't keep the negativity and insults from getting to me, no matter how hard I tried. It got to the point where I wasn't able to hold back my tears until after meetings anymore. I found myself wiping tears from my face right there in the meetings, hoping that nobody would notice; then I'd go home after work and cry myself to sleep. On days like that, I thought seriously about leaving Uber. I even applied for several other jobs. But, ultimately, I decided to stay. I was twenty-five years old. Uber was the third company I'd worked at since I graduated from Penn only a year and a half earlier. How could I convince the companies I applied to that the problem was with Uber, and not with me? Even worse, what if Kevin and Duncan were right, I'd wonder, and I was really an awful engineer? What if I was so awful that I would never get another job in engineering?

I wasn't the only person at Uber asking myself questions like these. Almost every other engineer I knew was going through the same issues. My coworkers who were being mistreated were white, black, Hispanic, Asian, male, female, gay, straight—*everyone*, I realized, was being bullied. One of my friends said his therapist was begging him to quit before something terrible happened. Another friend said that her manager (who was also a woman) refused to do anything about the homophobic abuse she suffered from a colleague, which made her feel like she—and not the abusive colleague—was the problem. Another said he applied for jobs elsewhere but did poorly in the interviews because, just like me, he couldn't get his manager's voice out of his head; "You *really* think you're an engineer?" the voice said, over and over again. Sometimes, my friends and I would go into an empty conference room, sit across from each other at the table, and discuss the things our managers were saying to us, then reassure each other they weren't true. "If we're really that terrible," we'd say, our voices faltering, "wouldn't they have given us terrible performance reviews or put us on performance improvement plans? Wouldn't they have fired us?"

Diversity had become a major issue for Uber, and I got the impression that many people within the company were trying very hard to fix the problem. Long before I arrived, Uber had instituted diversity and inclusion industry "best practices," and while I worked there, Uber checked all of the boxes for a company that cared about diversity and inclusion. It had mandatory unconscious bias, anti-harassment, and anti-discrimination training, and these training sessions were quite good, from what I remember. It had things like the bar-raiser program, which was aimed at eliminat-

ing bias and discrimination from the hiring process. It had hired
some of the most prominent and influential diversity and inclusion
advocates in the industry, empowered them to lead the charge on
diversity and inclusion issues, and actively hired from women's-
only software boot camps. It did culture and engagement surveys
regularly and tried to act on those surveys. It had employee re-
source groups for every gender, race, ethnicity, and sexual orientation. It had women on the board and had placed women in positions
of power throughout the company; the women in those positions
were not powerless, or tokens, or mere figureheads—I remember
very clearly the power that they had and how they chose to use it.
According to rumors I heard from managers and fellow colleagues,
the company even took diversity and inclusion into account for the
performance reviews, compensation, and bonuses of managers.

I'd believed in these initiatives during the first few months that
I worked at the company, but I quickly became disillusioned. The
issue wasn't that Uber needed to be more diverse and inclusive;
the issue was that Uber had a culture that ignored and violated
civil rights and employment laws. Uber didn't just need more
women engineers, or more employees of color; it needed to stop
breaking the law. As I sat in a LadyEng meeting one day that summer, listening to several of the women in the group talk about how
we all needed to help recruit more women and people of color, all
I could think was that it didn't matter how many women joined
the company, if those women were sexually harassed; that it didn't
matter how many black engineers we hired, if they were discriminated against; it didn't matter how many women we put into positions of power, if those women perpetrated or enabled the illegal

behavior. We weren't going to fix these systemic problems—
problems that were the reasons *why* we didn't have many engineers who were women or people of color—ourselves. These were
hugely complicated legal problems that the company was legally
obligated to address, yet refused to fix. Trying to repair Uber's
aggressive disregard for civil rights and employment laws with diversity and inclusion initiatives was like putting a Band-Aid on a
gunshot wound.

The company's systemic cultural problems—and especially its
sexism—were painfully obvious within SRE. That spring, after
Kevin came on board, I'd noticed that most of the other women
on our teams had either quit or transferred to other departments.
By the middle of the summer, the SRE team had gone from
25 percent women—the percentage that had helped persuade me
to join the company—to 6 percent. One day that summer, I stood
up at an engineering meeting attended by hundreds of people,
and asked David why so many women were leaving the company
and what Uber was doing about it. His response certainly answered my question: after saying that he made a point to "talk to
one woman every month," he speculated that perhaps if the
women at Uber were better engineers, then more women would
join the company. My face grew hot with anger. I couldn't believe
what I'd heard.

Rather than addressing the underlying issues that made women
want to transfer from certain teams or work somewhere else alto-
gether, our managers upped the pressure on the remaining women

engineers to recruit other women. Many of us already attended every "women in tech" networking event we could, and I now spent a great deal of time reaching out to other women on LinkedIn, Twitter, and GitHub, too. But I had no idea how far some managers would go to keep women on their teams and avoid being perceived as part of Uber's "diversity problem."

Mid-year performance reviews were approaching, and I knew that if I got a good review, Kevin and the SRE team would *have* to let me transfer. When I finally received my review, it was full of praise, and I let Kevin know that I would be transferring to another team. But when I went to request a transfer, he retroactively changed my review, giving me a lower performance score and saying that I showed no signs of an upward career trajectory. Horrified, I reported this to HR. The HR representative acknowledged that Kevin had broken company protocol and shouldn't have retroactively changed my review to keep me on his team, but refused to do anything about it. I was stuck.

I cried so hard that day. I cried in the bathroom at work and I cried at home. Not only would I still have to work for a manager who was cruel and abusive, but I found out that I couldn't take any more classes at Stanford because Uber would no longer sponsor me due to the new low performance review. I felt like my life was falling apart, like all of my dreams were crumbling; I was back at Penn all over again, losing my master's degree in philosophy, realizing I would never be a physicist, sitting on the bathroom floor in the David Rittenhouse Laboratory and crying, feeling completely powerless.

A few days after my transfer request was denied, I overheard

Kevin talking to other employees at a team dinner about the "diversity problem" at the company. Other engineering teams were "losing women left and right," he said, but he'd found a way to keep women on his team. I looked around the table, at each of the women who were on one of his teams. As my glance passed each one, I tried to remember anything and everything she'd told me about her performance review. As I recalled our conversations, I realized that some of them had recently tried to transfer to other teams, just like me. And yet here we all were, still on Kevin's teams. That's when it hit me: It wasn't just me. He had prevented us all from transferring to other teams—all as part of a systematic scheme to preserve his "diversity numbers."

After the summer performance review season came to a close, I came into work one day to learn that one of my coworkers, a black man named Joseph Thomas who had been bullied by his managers, was dead. I later learned that he'd shot himself in his car and, by the time his wife found him, it was too late. Before he committed suicide, he had told one of his friends that Uber was breaking him down. "The sad thing is this place (Uber) has broken me to the point where I don't have the strength to look for another job,"* his friend told the *San Francisco Chronicle*, repeating his words. As his widow, Zecole, told the reporter, "It's hard to explain, but he

---

* Carolyn Said, "Suicide of an Uber Engineer: Widow Blames Job Stress," *San Francisco Chronicle*, April 25, 2017.

wasn't himself at all. . . . He'd say things like, 'My boss doesn't like me.' His personality changed totally; he was horribly concerned about his work, to the point it was almost unbelievable. He was saying he couldn't do anything right."

Immediately after his death, one of the engineering directors sent our department an email in which he wrongly said that Joseph Thomas had died in a car accident. I wanted to believe him, but I couldn't find any records of the supposed car accident. I suspected it was suicide, because I knew what Uber did to people. Many of my coworkers were having suicidal thoughts, and, earlier that year, another Uber employee had attempted suicide after being harassed and discriminated against. Thankfully, this person survived, but it shook us. "It could have been me," several colleagues whispered. "It *should* have been me," one coworker said. And, I said to myself, "It almost *was* me."

I remembered standing on the BART platform one morning earlier that summer, on my way to work. I'd angered my managers the day before, and I knew that I'd have to meet with them that afternoon. I knew that I'd be reprimanded and berated, knew that I'd have to defend myself again. As the train approached the platform, I looked at the tracks, and a terrible thought crossed my mind: *I would rather be dead than go into work again.* For a moment, I considered stepping off the platform and lying down on the rails. I started to cry, standing there on the platform, and tried to wipe the tears away from my face as the train pulled into the station.

After Joseph's suicide, I felt like I had woken up from a terrible, horrifying dream. The problem wasn't me or any of Uber's other low-level employees but Uber's culture—a culture created and sustained by multiple levels of executives and managers who gradually, cruelly ground employees down until they felt that life was no longer worth living. I was determined not to be the next victim, determined that Joseph Thomas's suicide would be the last.

CHAPTER NINE

In the days that followed, I worked hard to regain my confidence and shut out the voices that told me I was worthless, that I wasn't a "real engineer," that I was a fraud. I began spending even more time with Chad and my friends, who brought me happiness and gave me the encouragement, support, and love that I so desperately needed. I started a blog, which gave me an outlet to share my thoughts about physics, life, books, and engineering. I went back to the Stoics and tried to replace Kevin's cruel insults with the words of Seneca, Epictetus, and Marcus Aurelius. Every morning, as I walked to the North Berkeley BART station, I began my workday by reading this famous passage from Marcus Aurelius's *Meditations*: "Say to yourself first thing in the morning: today I shall meet people who are meddling, ungrateful, aggressive, treacherous, malicious, unsocial. All this has afflicted them through their ignorance of true good and evil. But I have seen that the nature of good is what is right, and the nature of evil what is wrong." I read these words again and again, until I internalized them; I told myself that the managers at Uber who treated me and my colleagues poorly did so because they didn't know that what they were doing was wrong.

The words of the Stoics reinforced what I already knew: I couldn't control what others did to me, but I could control how I reacted. I was the only person who could control my own character—the things that made me who I was, the things that defined me. Hell-bent on finding myself again, determined to become the best version of myself that I could be, I spent a little bit of time every evening holding myself accountable. In my journals, I wrote down the things I had done wrong that day, the things I had done right, and everything I could have done better. I did what Benjamin Franklin had done as a young man, and made a list of the virtues I wanted to develop and practice every day: patience, kindness, generosity, compassion, love, justice—these, and not what anyone at work said about me, would be the yardsticks by which I measured my character. With each passing day, I felt a little less powerless, a little less afraid, a little more free.

On particularly rough days, I'd read quotations from Fred Rogers, whose gentleness was, at times, the only thing that made me feel like my life was going to be okay. The thing he wrote that gave me the most courage was this: "Try your best to make goodness attractive. That's one of the toughest assignments you'll ever be given." I made up my mind that even though goodness was considered a vice at Uber, and aggression considered its greatest virtue, I would still care about goodness, about kindness, about gentleness. I was determined to bring those virtues into work every single day, into every one of my meetings, into every moment of my life. I would be *in* the world, but I certainly wouldn't be *of* it—just as my father had counseled, all those years ago.

It wasn't easy. Whenever people at work insulted me, I had to keep my cool; I'd take a deep breath and tell myself that they were merely ignorant of the fact that what they were doing was wrong. But my renewed Stoicism wasn't just about turning the other cheek. It also came with responsibility: as someone who knew what was right and wrong, the Stoics taught, I was obligated to always do what was right.

I began calling out sexism, racism, and bullying when they happened, just as I had back when I was a bar raiser. If I noticed someone being a bully toward others, I brought it up to management and insisted that they take action to stop it. Every time something ridiculous happened, every time a sexist email was sent, I'd send a short report to HR, just to keep a record going. When coworkers came to me for help, I tried my best to coach them on how to address the mistreatment they received from sexist and racist managers, how to document discrimination, how to escalate things to HR, how to escalate things to Uber's executives, and—when that failed—how to escalate things to government and legal authorities (by contacting, for example, the EEOC).

On days when I felt afraid, when I was worried for my coworkers or my job or my mental health, I would open my copy of Epictetus's *Enchiridion* on the BART ride home. "When you have decided that a thing ought to be done, and are doing it, never avoid being seen doing it, though the many shall form an unfavor-able opinion about it," Epictetus said. "For if it is not right to do it, avoid doing the thing; but if it is right, why are you afraid of those who shall find fault wrongly?" His words gave me courage to stand up against the bullying from Uber's management. On really bad days, I would pull the book out in between meetings, reading as I walked up and down the halls of Uber's headquarters, some-times walking past Travis Kalanick, who would be pacing around the building, talking on his phone.

I started to feel that I had more control over my life. By defin-ing myself in terms of my character—which was completely in my power—instead of letting my managers define me, I was able to slowly repair my sense of self-worth. Though the way I and others were being treated didn't change, I was managing to weather the abuse better, to remain focused on my work, to begin planning for and dreaming of a life after Uber. As always, there was plenty to do: software architecture to review, microservices to fix, code to debug, new engineers to teach, colleagues to help. In the evenings, I worked on my microservices book, hoping I could put it all to-gether in time for its scheduled Christmas publication date.

Back in the summer, Uber had announced that it was buying cus-tomized leather jackets for everyone in SRE. It was a tradition that several of the engineering directors had brought with them from Google. (Another tradition they brought with them was a heavy drinking culture, where engineers were expected to drink whiskey regularly with their managers and directors; anyone who didn't join in the drinking was considered not dedicated to the team.) We all went to conference rooms where there were sample jackets for us to try on; we picked out our sizes, and waited for the jackets to arrive.

One day, as September was coming to an end, I received an email. The email had been sent to 8 women: the 6 remaining women in the infrastructure engineering organization (which included SRE and had a total of 150 engineers) and 2 women who'd recently transferred to different departments within the company. Uber, the email announced, would not be buying leather jackets for the women engineers, because there were not enough women to justify placing the order; the company was, however, ordering leather jackets for all of the men. I replied to the email, doing my best to point out how ridiculous this decision was. "There are 8 women in SRE," I wrote. "I'm sure SRE can find room in the budget to afford leather jackets for the women, especially since it can afford them for the men."

Charles replied that Uber had gotten a bulk discount on the men's jackets, but because there were only a few women, the company hadn't been able to get the same discount for the women's. Spending $100 more for each woman's jacket would be unfair to the men, he argued, so the women would not be receiving jackets unless Uber found jackets that were the exact same price as the men's. Given the large discount on the men's jackets, this was obviously impossible. I replied again, trying to explain why this was unfair: "Considering that the cost associated with rectifying this inequality is quite low ($100 each) and that the money saved by the bulk order of men's jackets more than covers the small additional cost of the women's jackets, I do hope that SRE can find room in the budget to ensure that all SREs are included as part of the team and can wear their Uber SRE jackets with pride."

"If you still continue to have the perception of inequality," Charles replied, "I don't think email is a good medium to address this—please schedule some 1:1 time with me to discuss your concerns." I forwarded the email thread to HR and closed my laptop.

I messaged Laura, who had also received the email, and asked her to meet me on the quietest floor of the engineering office. We sat down together on a gigantic black beanbag chair and burst into laughter. It was an absurd situation, filled with such ridiculously blatant, banal sexism, that neither of us could believe it was really happening. We pulled up the email on our phones, read it to each other aloud, and laughed until we had tears in our eyes. But before we parted ways and returned to our work, there was a moment of understanding, and we grew quiet. I think we both knew that this was the beginning of the end for us at Uber. It was now clear that the company held its female engineers in such disregard that it could not even be bothered to *pretend* to treat them as equals to their male peers and that the culture would never change, no matter how hard we tried to change it. For the very first time, we talked about what would happen if I shared the story of the real Uber with the world.

The idea of sharing my story seemed dangerous but inevitable. My entire life had been shaped by the things I'd read; it was the stories of others that had brought me here, that had given me the courage and determination to pull myself out of poverty and take my fate into my own hands. There was no question in my mind that I would one day write about what had happened at Uber, even though the thought of doing so completely terrified me. As Laura and I discussed it for the very first time, I found that talking about it made it seem a little less frightening.

Several days later, I met with yet another HR representative, whose name was Jan, to discuss the leather jackets and my emails with Charles—or so I thought. We met at the top floor of Uber's head-quarters, where I'd never been before. The walls were lined with windows that framed a beautiful, nearly 360-degree view of San Francisco, and there were mini golf stations set up around the desks.

Jan intimidated me from the moment I saw her. She was very tall and wore five-inch stilettos that made her a good foot taller than me. Once she introduced herself, I realized that it wasn't her height that made me feel small; rather, it was the way she looked down at me with an exasperated frown and raised her eyebrows when I spoke, as if to ask, "Are you finished talking yet?"

As we walked into the conference room, I tried to collect my-self, preparing to explain to her why this situation was ridiculous, but Jan had something else in store for me.

"Have you ever considered," she asked with a smirk, in an almost-British accent that I couldn't quite place, "that *you* might be the problem here at Uber?"

I balked. "No, no," I said, stammering, "look at Charles's email; I clearly wasn't the problem there, and . . ."

"Well," she said, interrupting me, "the way I see it, all the complaints you've made to HR have one thing in common, and that thing *is you*."

Before I had a chance to reply, she urged me to consider looking closely at my life, encouraged me to ask myself what I had done to make these terrible things happen at Uber. Then she leaned back in her chair and cocked her head to one side, looking down her nose at me.

I told her that I *had*, in fact, looked very closely at my life, but this wasn't about my life or really about me at all; it was about Uber. "Everything I've reported to HR," I said, growing frustrated, "was a serious, well-documented incident, and many of these situations had nothing to do with me."

"What incidents are you referring to?" she asked, a confused and impatient look on her face. "I have access to all the complaints in HR," she continued, "and you've never made any complaints before."

I felt like I was losing my mind. I pointed out that she'd just referred to my prior complaints, and spoken of terrible things that had happened at Uber, when she said that all of the complaints I had made to HR had *me* in common. She shook her head and insisted that she didn't know what I was talking about.

"Here," I said, reaching for my laptop. "I'll pull up all the emails that I've sent to HR. And I'm not the only one who has reported these things to you; other women have reported them too."

This caught her attention. "How did you know," she asked, sitting upright in her chair and leaning toward me, "that other women reported things to HR?" She asked me how women at Uber communicated with one another, which chat rooms we talked in, what we talked about, and if we ever talked about sexism and sexual harassment. I refused to tell her. Hoping to bring the conversation back to the jackets, I mentioned how few women were left in my engineering department. "Some people," she said with a sigh, "see sexism and racism in places where there really isn't any." Then she told me a story.

Several years ago, she said, she worked at an accounting firm. "They thought we had a diversity problem," she continued, shaking her head in apparent disappointment, "because all of the accountants were female Asians." But, she said, what people didn't understand was that the firm didn't *really* have a diversity problem, because "female Asians" were "good with numbers" and because "being good with numbers" was just "what *they* do." It wasn't sexism or racism, she insisted; it was just the truth. Similarly, she concluded, white men were just really "good at engineering." I wanted to point out—among other things—that the majority of men in our engineering department were Asian, not white, but I held my tongue.

As our meeting came to an end, she berated me for reporting the jackets email to HR, saying it was unprofessional and inappropriate for me to ever discuss these things over email. She cautioned me to never report things to HR over email again. It was, she said, a violation of Uber's cultural values: according to "Principled Confrontation," if you had a problem with someone, you were supposed to talk to him or her in person. As I stood up to leave, I tried to point out that she had contradicted herself again, because she had just, several minutes ago, insisted that I had never reported anything to HR. Furthermore, I argued, if I hadn't ever reported anything over email, I would have no record of the things that had happened. She brushed me off and said she'd be in touch.

Violating "Principled Confrontation" yet again, I sent an email to the head of HR in which I summarized my conversation with Jan. In the message, after recounting Jan's racist anecdote, I asked (only half-jokingly), "How do I report HR to HR?"

Around the same time, Jan sent me an email following up on our conversation and asking for information about the other women who had made complaints to HR. In her email signature was a quotation from Montaigne: "We need very strong ears to hear ourselves judged frankly, and because there are few who can endure frank criticism without being stung by it, those who venture to criticize us perform a remarkable act of friendship, for to undertake to wound or offend a man for his own good is to have a healthy love for him." I wondered if she considered what she and Uber were doing to their employees a "remarkable act of friendship," if the treatment that had pushed Joseph Thomas to his suicide was something she saw as having been done "for his own good."

A few days later, Kevin pulled me aside for a meeting. We sat down in one of the small conference rooms, and I began to talk about a software architecture project I was working on, but he raised his hands to interrupt me.

"Susan," he said, his face turning red, "we need to have a difficult conversation." We looked at each other for a moment, neither of us wanting to be the first to speak. He started to sweat, and after wiping the sweat from his face onto his sleeve, leaving a series of wet streaks across his arms, he said that we needed to talk about the email chain with Charles that I'd forwarded to HR. "You're on very thin ice for reporting this to HR," he said, wiping the sweat from his face again. "California is an at-will state, so we can fire you if you ever do anything like this again." I shook my head and replied that it was illegal for Uber to fire me for reporting things to HR. He disagreed, citing his experience at Google. "I've been a manager for a *really* long time, Susan," he replied, "and if *that* was illegal, I would know about it."

A few days later, the women of SRE received an email announcing that the leather jackets had arrived. I went upstairs and waited in line with the other engineers as the jackets were handed out. As I made my way through the line, one of the managers passed by, his own embroidered jacket in hand. "I hope you're happy," he sneered.

On my way home that night, I walked down the street to the BART station and shoved my Uber-branded leather jacket into the trash. I was fuming. It had never been about the jackets; it was about the bullying, the harassment, the discrimination, and the retaliation that my colleagues and I were constantly subjected to. It had never been about the jackets, but the threats, the fear, and the abuse from management. Keeping the jacket felt wrong. It felt like holding on to it and (God forbid) wearing it meant approving of Uber's behavior and being complicit in its mistreatment of employees and its attempts to whitewash that mistreatment. Riding the BART train home, crammed like a sardine in a can with all the other commuters heading toward the East Bay, I realized that staying at Uber was just like keeping the jacket. Staying meant, in some twisted way, that I approved of the way Uber treated me and my colleagues. Staying made me complicit, made me part of the problem. Unless the company drastically changed in the coming months, I would have to leave Uber.

I didn't have much time to think about what to do next. I was working ten to twelve hours a day, trying to finish up my book, teaching Engucation classes, and giving talks at conferences on microservice architecture and how to build better software systems. Then something wonderful happened: Chad proposed to me.

It was a beautiful, warm, sunny October afternoon. I was working in the Berkeley pumpkin house, writing my book about microservices and waiting for Chad to stop by in his old beige BMW and drive us up to our favorite hiking trail in Tilden Park. Just before he arrived, he texted me and asked me if I'd like a coffee for the hike. I was tired, having written all day and long into the night before, so I told him I'd love one. After he picked me up and as we drove through Berkeley and up into the Berkeley Hills, I felt like something was different—it seemed like he had something on his mind, something he wanted to say but was holding back.

Once we got to Tilden, we walked up one of our favorite trails. It went deep into the hills, through small streams and creeks and beneath enormous pines and eucalyptus trees. I drank almost all of my coffee, and didn't notice that he hadn't had a single sip of his. We walked and talked all the way up the trail, until we got to our favorite spot, a place beneath a beautiful oak tree where you could look out toward the west and see Berkeley, the beautiful San Francisco Bay, the towers of downtown San Francisco, Marin, and the Golden Gate Bridge in the distance. We stopped to rest, and Chad turned to me.

"Will you marry me?" he asked.

I wasn't sure if he was really asking me or not. I looked in his sweet, handsome face, and at his nervous smile. *I wish he was asking me for real,* I thought to myself. "I'll marry you any day," I said, before giving him a kiss.

"No, I'm serious, Susan Joy," he exclaimed. He pulled the lid off of his coffee cup, then reached inside and pulled out a ring. He got down on his knees, right beneath the little oak tree, as the cool evening breeze blew in from the bay, and asked, "Will you marry me?"

I burst into tears and said, "Yes."

We'd been dating for nearly a year, and I'd fallen head over heels in love with him. He was the kind of person I'd always dreamed of marrying—brilliant, technical, artistic, sweet, and fun—and, somehow, he'd fallen in love with me, too. While I'd been dragging myself through my year at Uber, he'd also been working hard: he had grown his company to nearly sixty people, raised tens of millions of dollars in funding, and built real qubits that actually worked. While I navigated the challenges of working at a tech company, he was navigating the challenges of running and building one; we leaned on each other, talking through every issue and challenge during our long walks through Tilden Park. We were a perfect team, and now that we were going to be married, we would be partners for life.

It was through my conversations with Chad that I realized I'd lost all patience with Uber, that it was time to move on. I was tired of being the victim in the story of my life, tired of waiting for things to change, angry that I'd once again let myself become the object, rather than the subject, of my own life. I was smart, I was hardworking, I was engaged to the man of my dreams, and I could do just about anything I set my mind to. I deserved better than Uber, I deserved better than what Silicon Valley had given me, and I was ready for something more. But then, just when I'd made up my mind that I would leave, a glimmer of hope appeared.

In mid-October, Uber had sponsored the Grace Hopper Conference. Many of the women from LadyEng had traveled to Houston for the conference, to staff the Uber booth and to recruit young women for software engineering positions. Uber's CTO, Thuan Pham, was also in attendance. At a dinner during the conference, one of the women had told Thuan that there was a serious problem at Uber: managers within the engineering group had been giving their female employees low performance scores—and, in particularly egregious cases, changing their performance scores *after* the performance review cycle had ended—in order to keep their "diversity numbers" from falling. Addressing the women in attendance, Thuan said he knew that this was a problem at Uber and urged them to tell anyone who had experienced this treatment to come meet with him immediately so that he could take action.

When she returned from Houston, Laura—who had attended the dinner—pulled me aside and encouraged me to meet with Thuan. I wasn't so sure—after all, I clearly remembered the way he had ignored the problems that Ashley brought to him only a few months earlier—but Laura was earnest and excited. He had assured her, she said, that if I met with him and explained everything that had happened, he would fix things. The more we talked about it, the more excited I felt: Maybe change was still possible, maybe things would turn around, and I wouldn't have to leave. At the very least, I owed it to myself, and to my fellow employees, to give it a try.

I soon found myself back at the top floor of Uber's headquarters, where I'd recently met with Jan. Once again, I sat on the fabric sofa near the conference rooms while I waited for our meeting to start, looking at the little putting greens with their artificial grass, watching members of the executive staff stand by the windows overlooking the city, chatting with one another with their coffees and their cans of La Croix. As soon as our assigned conference room was free, I walked in to meet Uber's famous CTO, Thuan Pham, and sat down across from him. As the door closed, I noticed that there were pieces of gray duct tape stretched across the latch and deadbolt, preventing the door from locking.

I started from the beginning. When I brought up the chat messages I received from Jake during my first days at Uber, he said that he remembered the incident and was sorry that it had happened to me. When I told him about my transfer requests being blocked and my performance review being changed, and how that had resulted in my losing my spot in the Stanford program, he said he was "pissed." When I explained what had happened with the jackets, Charles's response, the meeting with Jan, and how Kevin had threatened my job, he sounded outraged.

He was not surprised by any of the stories I told him, he said, but he was angry about them. He knew there was a serious systemic problem in Uber's engineering teams, that male managers were giving their female engineers low performance reviews and preventing them from transferring to other teams in order to protect their diversity numbers. In fact, he said, he'd just fired one male manager on the money team for doing this to one of the female engineers. He promised me that he would take care of it and that I would be hearing from one of his HR liaisons very soon.

In all of my time at Uber, I'd never felt so hopeful as I did when I left that meeting. Every other time I had met with managers or HR representatives, they'd gaslighted me, trying to convince me that *I* was the problem. But here, for the first time, someone at Uber had agreed with me that what Uber was doing to its employees was wrong, and he had promised to fix it. I was optimistic, but a nagging voice in the back of my head cautioned me to be careful, reminding me of the last two times I had met with someone in a position of power and had felt this way, and how those situations had turned out: first, with the dean of graduate studies at Penn, who promised to fix everything but instead pulled my master's degree out from under me; then, with Karen during my first days at Uber, who promised to fix everything but instead retaliated against me for reporting Jake for sexual harassment. There was a good chance that what Thuan had promised was too good to be true. I'd have to wait and see.

Later that same day, Thuan forwarded me an email that he had sent to his engineering managers a few days before. "Earlier today, we terminated the employment of a manager," the email said, referring to the manager from the money team he'd brought up in our meeting, who had been fired for changing a female engineer's performance review, "because this person did not treat his team members with care and respect, did not create an environment for members of his team to do their best work, and generally acted against our liberal engineering transfer policy." He went on, "This is also an indication that we have failed some of our employees in some parts of the organization. We have said over and over again that we have zero tolerance for bad managers, and yet we still have some in our midst."

At the top of the email, he'd written me a personal note, thanking me for meeting with him and saying that he and the head of HR would "thoroughly investigate all the concerns" that I had raised. He promised me I would not be fired "without [his] knowledge and approval" and that the way that managers at Uber were speaking to their employees was "completely destructive and intimidating, and simply not acceptable." He ended the note by asking me to tell my engineering friends "that we do not tolerate bad management behaviors. And if they see bad stuff, please be courageous to help us out by coming to tell HR and me directly. It's totally safe."

I waited, eager and impatient, to hear from Thuan's HR liaison. In the meantime, I tried to avoid meeting with Kevin, afraid that he'd fire me as soon as he realized I'd reported what he'd done to the CTO. I told Laura about my meeting with Thuan, and together we wondered what he would do—whether he would take action, whether things at Uber would really change. Then we waited. While we were waiting, we received the news that Charles had received an offer from Google, and he left Uber and joined Google as a high-level director of engineering.

I soon heard from Thuan's "HR liaison," an HR representative named Toby, who scheduled a meeting with me. I'd met Toby briefly before, over a videoconference call, after I'd reported Jan's behavior in our meeting to the head of HR. He had called to explain that Uber would not be taking any disciplinary action against Jan for what she'd said in our meeting; they'd substantiated everything I'd reported, he said, but because Jan was new and it was her first offense, they didn't feel comfortable giving her much more than a stern warning. In other words, he just repeated the same HR script I'd heard every time I had reported something to HR in the past. Still, when Toby and I scheduled our meeting to follow up on my conversation with Thuan, I felt hopeful. In retrospect, I don't know *why*, but I really believed that this time things would finally be different.

And then I sat there, across a gray conference table from Toby, and listened as he explained that Uber had investigated the things I had reported to Thuan. While it was true that Kevin had blocked my transfer and had given me a retaliatory performance review because I was a woman and he wanted to keep me on his team, and while it was true that Kevin had threatened to fire me for reporting sexism to HR, and while it was true that all of this was illegal, Kevin was a high performer, this was his first offense, and they didn't feel comfortable punishing him. I burst into tears.

"What am I supposed to do?" I asked, wiping the tears from my face.

"I'm sorry," he said, shaking his head.

"You can't—you won't—do anything?" I asked. "I get threatened, and I get my performance review changed, and you won't do anything? What am I supposed to do?"

"I don't know," he said quietly. "I'm so sorry."

"What am I supposed to do," I pleaded, "if something else happens? If something worse happens?"

He told me that if anything else happened, I should report it to HR and let HR investigate and take disciplinary action.

"No, thank you, but no," I said, growing angry. I wiped the hot tears from my face again and looked up at him. Our eyes met. I saw that his eyes were red, and he looked like he was about to cry. It struck me then that perhaps he was just as powerless, just as stuck in the Uber machine, as I was. The anger I felt toward him went away.

"I'm sorry," he said again. I knew he meant it.

I thanked him and left. I didn't go back to the office, didn't return to my desk, didn't check my emails, didn't turn on the company chat app on my phone. I went home, had a cigarette, sat on my bed, and started looking for a new job.

I had made up my mind on the way home that I would never again accept a job in which I was a low-level employee, in which I was powerless. This meant I could no longer work in engineering, because the only software engineering jobs that I was qualified for were junior- and mid-level roles, roles that would put me at the mercy of yet another line manager who would have far too much control over my work and my life. I loved engineering, but I loved myself more, and I was determined to find work that was technical and challenging but that still allowed me to determine my own destiny.

Less than a week later, I was offered a job as the founding editor in chief of the payment startup Stripe's new software engineering magazine. Patrick Collison, Stripe's CEO, had come across a blog post I'd written about books that had changed my life. He seemed impressed by that blog post—and the other things I'd written—and he wanted me to come work for him. It was the absolutely perfect job for me, and I accepted.

When Patrick offered me the job, I realized that it was a chance for me to finally realize my childhood dream and work full-time as a writer and editor. Writing the microservices book had been a trial run for me, one in which I could find out if I really wanted to be a writer and if I really had what it took to be one. I was pleasantly surprised to discover that I absolutely loved writing the book, that I couldn't wait to sit down at my laptop with my notes and notebooks and write and revise and write and revise *ad infinitum* until the early hours of the morning. When I told Chad about the job at Stripe, he was just as excited as I was; he loved my writing and encouraged me to pursue it as a career. Shortly after our engagement, I left the orange house and moved into Chad's little apartment in Emeryville, just south of Berkeley. The apartment had one bedroom and a little den upstairs, next to the kitchen, that Chad had turned into his office. When I moved in, he moved his desk and all of his things into the living room and gave the office to me. "It's for your writing," he said.

I didn't want to leave Uber without offering an account, in writing, of the way I'd been treated there and the problems I'd observed in the culture, so I sat down and wrote a letter of resignation. I wrote that I was sad to be leaving Uber. I was thankful for all that I had learned there, for the amazing opportunities I had been offered, and for all of the extraordinary people I had worked with. However, I had decided to leave because I could no longer accept the inappropriate and demoralizing ways that I and some of my fellow engineers had been treated. After the many instances of sexism, abuse, and retaliation I'd experienced and witnessed, I couldn't stay at the company and continue to allow myself to be treated so poorly. I could no longer speak positively about Uber when asked if it was a good place to work, could no longer in good conscience encourage women to join Uber SRE. Finally, I said that I hoped that Uber would make some significant cultural changes in the future so that there wouldn't be any more experiences like my own.

I tried to schedule a meeting with Kevin so that I could give him my letter of resignation in person, but he refused to see me and attempted to push our meeting into the future. Because it was nearing the end of the year, I couldn't help but wonder if this was just another tactic he was trying to use to keep his diversity numbers up and get one of the "diversity bonuses" I'd heard so much about, so I emailed the head of HR and asked to meet with one of their representatives instead.

In a rather surreal meeting, it was Jan who accepted my resignation. As we went over my tenure at Uber and I covered the events and systemic cultural problems and illegal practices that had led to my resignation, Jan periodically interrupted me, encouraging me to "learn" from my experiences at Uber. She desperately hoped, she said, that I wouldn't make the same mistakes at my next job. I had no energy left with which to disagree with her. I had nothing left to say.

On my very last day in the office, HR diverted me away from the prescheduled exit interview and sent me back to the so-called harassment task force—right back to Jessica, the woman who, when a number of us had joined together to come forward about Jake, had falsely told me that everyone else was there to complain about me. As we sat across from each other for the last time, she repeated the same thing she'd said to me the last time we had spoken. "I thought you were happy with the way we've handled things," she said. I started to go over the entire history of my year at Uber yet again, but it was no use. She seemed unable to comprehend that Uber had done anything wrong.

After our meeting, I pulled up the company directory and calculated the percentage of women who were still on my engineering team; there were over 150 engineers in the site reliability engineering department, and only 3 percent were women. On my way out, I handed in my laptop and my Uber badge. As I left the building, I walked through the office and said goodbye to all of my closest friends. I passed the desks where I once sat, the conference rooms and tables and seating areas where all of the drama had played out. I met Laura in one of the kitchens, and we stood there together for the last time, talking about what was next.

"You're going to write about it, aren't you?" she asked with a smile.

CHAPTER **TEN**

I took a few weeks off for Christmas—going skiing and snowshoeing with Chad and his family; going home to Arizona to spend time with mine—then started my new job at Stripe in January 2017. After working in Uber's intense, aggressive, destructive environment, I found that working at Stripe was quite a culture shock. At Uber, every meeting had been a short, painful skirmish, where managers and employees fought like starving dogs over a scrap of meat. But Stripe seemed very different. My colleagues were friendly, kind, and collaborative; the people I reported to in my new role treated me with respect and empowered me; and I was pleasantly surprised when I walked into meetings and found everyone smiling, laughing, and having fun, excited to share the things they'd worked on. At Uber, every conversation, every interaction, had been about power; at Stripe, power rarely seemed to enter anyone's mind.

The Collison brothers—Patrick (Stripe's CEO) and John (the company's president)—largely gave me and my team free rein to do whatever we needed to turn the dream of the magazine (which we'd decided to call *Increment*) into a real, beautiful print and digital publication that people in the tech industry would love to read. I knew it wasn't going to be an easy job—starting a print and digital publication from scratch was no joke, especially for someone without any media experience. And I'd been given a short deadline: I had to scrape together a full issue of *Increment* in just two months.

But I found that I was thankful for the challenge, grateful for the intensity. It was a dark time in the world. Donald Trump had just been elected president, and no one really knew what to expect. Everyone seemed angry and uncertain, and there was a palpable sense of fear, unrest, and suspense in the air. There were rumors that Russia had influenced the election, and many believed that Trump himself was linked to Russia. I didn't know what would happen. I didn't know if we would soon be at war, if our economy would collapse, if the rumors about his links to Russia were true.

I had spent most of my life too wrapped up in my personal struggles to pay much attention to everything happening in the world around me. My life had been largely untouched by politics, and I had taken it for granted, forgetting that a functioning democracy required the involvement of its citizens. I had always naively assumed, for better or for worse, that things would sort themselves out, that the people running the country—with rare exceptions—knew what they were doing. In the wake of Trump's election, as the entire country went into a tailspin, all of my illusions unraveled. I felt a gnawing in my soul, felt very strongly that the world was not someone else's problem anymore but that it was mine. I think other people felt this, too; things we had once thought of as "someone else's problem" were now problems that every one of us was acutely, painfully aware of and responsible for. I felt that I needed to do something, something that would make the world better and less angry as it grew more confusing, more polarized, more furious.

When I think of those first months of Trump's presidency, that's what I remember most: the anger. At times it seemed that anger was the only thing that liberals and conservatives had in common. Everyone was angry. Everyone was looking for someone to jump on, to correct, to censure, to shun, to destroy. Everyone was looking for someone to blame.

I wanted to leave Uber behind, but doing so turned out to be impossible. When I handed in my resignation, I expected that the heavy, depressing weight I carried with me would lift and disappear, but it didn't. I expected, anticipated, and hoped for relief, but the heaviness in my heart only grew with each passing day. "I'll start to feel better any day now," I would tell myself. "If not today, then maybe tomorrow." But I never felt any better; I only ever felt worse.

I couldn't escape Uber—it followed me everywhere. My immediate family and my closest friends knew what had happened there, and they didn't question me about why I left; if anything, they wondered why it had taken me so long to leave. But my new coworkers, my extended family, and many of my friends wanted to know why I had left one of the most successful startups in the world. Several journalists called me up, asking me why I left, hoping that I would tell them something they didn't already know. I never knew what to say. How, I wondered, could I ever possibly explain everything that had happened? Where would I even start?

Then, one day, Uber was back in the headlines. At the end of January, President Trump issued Executive Order 13769, known as the Muslim ban, which prohibited nationals from seven predominantly Muslim countries from entering the United States. This created an immediate crisis at airports across the United States; people from these countries—even those who had American visas and green cards—were stranded and detained in the confusion. Protests broke out, and demonstrators, lawyers, and politicians rushed to the airports.

Amid the chaos, taxi drivers in New York City went on strike, refusing to pick up passengers from Kennedy Airport in protest against the ban. Drivers for Lyft joined them in solidarity. Uber, however, didn't participate in the strike. There was an uproar, and the #DeleteUber hashtag began to trend on Twitter. In the early days of #DeleteUber, an estimated 200,000 users deleted their accounts—a number that continued to grow as Twitter and the media covered Uber's connections to the Trump administration. Alongside other CEOs like Elon Musk, Travis Kalanick had joined Trump's economic advisory council shortly after the election; now, in light of the Muslim ban, Uber's employees and customers were pressuring him to resign. Faced with growing employee unrest and unhappy users, Kalanick resigned from the council. #DeleteUber stopped trending.

In the weeks that followed, Uber's performance review season kicked into high gear. I was still in touch with many of my friends

there, and every story they told me was another familiar nightmare. Several of my male colleagues had been yelled at by their
managers until they broke down in tears. Another coworker was
so shaken by what he'd overheard managers saying about their
employees that he threw up in a wastebasket in one of the conference rooms. Women from LadyEng were still experiencing the
same transfer-blocking song and dance I'd gone through, despite Thuan's being aware of, and having promised to rectify, the
problem.

I watched as one by one my friends were beaten down until
they reached their breaking points. I heard it in their voices, that
same despair and self-loathing that I myself had felt, the same despair and self-loathing I'd heard in the voices of my coworkers
who had reached suicidal levels of depression only six months earlier. Their attitudes wavered between resignation and anger. "I'm
going to fight it," they would say one day. "Uber can't keep treat-
ing people like this." Then, a few days later, after another meeting
with their managers, they would always come back to me and say
the opposite. "I can't fight anymore," they would say, defeated.
"I'm too tired, I can't do this anymore, I want to give up. I have to
give up." Sometimes, they would ask the question I was always
trying to dodge, the question I was unable to ask myself: "When
are you going to write something?"

Again, I didn't know what to say. I hoped that one of the journalists I had spoken to would write about it, but it didn't sound
like they would (or could) without my friends and coworkers at
Uber also going on the record—something that nobody was willing to do at the time. I knew I would have to tell my story eventually;

there was never any question of whether I would do it, only a question of how long it would take me to overcome my fear. I knew what happened to whistleblowers, what happened to women who spoke out about harassment, what happened to low-level employees who went up against multibillion-dollar corporations, what happened to former Uber employees who tried to speak out about the company. I was afraid to tell my story, and I hated admitting that I was afraid. Whenever thoughts of my own inaction began to weigh on my conscience, I pushed them away. "Not today," I told myself. "Maybe tomorrow, but not today."

I threw myself into my work, hoping that it would distract me. I assembled the best team I could, bringing together brilliant graphic designers and engineers and managers and marketers, and together we worked day and night to bring *Increment* to life. Because I didn't have a moment to spare, I made decisions quickly: we'd release issues quarterly, we'd release them in print and online, we'd group them by themes; we'd try to cover things that were evergreen and not merely news stories, and we'd make the magazine so beautiful that you couldn't help but turn its pages. I called up editors of small and large print magazines and learned from their mistakes and their triumphs; I took long walks through the city with tech journalists and editors who shared their hard-earned lessons.

I had a long list of themes I wanted to cover in my new magazine—everything from biotech to deep learning, from fundraising and hiring software engineers to serverless architecture—

and narrowing it down was difficult. Eventually, I landed on the topic of on-call best practices, because I knew that even in the worst-case scenario where nobody else could write for the magazine, the engineering team at Stripe and I could put something together pretty quickly. As it turned out, persuading experienced journalists to jump in and write for an inexperienced editor at a brand-new magazine that was being financed and run by a Silicon Valley tech company turned out to be pretty difficult; everyone wanted to see an issue of the magazine before they wrote an article for it. Ryn Daniels, a gifted infrastructure engineer and a fellow O'Reilly author, jumped in and wrote about creating sustainable on-call rotations, but they were the only non-Stripe employee to write a piece. We scrambled to put the rest of the issue together: Will Larson, one of the engineering managers at Stripe (and one of my old coworkers from Uber), wrote about scaling on-call practices; I got on the phone with GitLab's CEO, Sid Sijbrandij, and interviewed him about GitLab's recent outage; I interviewed engineers at over thirty companies about how they approached on call, and put their answers together to write the three remaining pieces.

At the same time, Chad and I were planning our wedding. We had originally planned for a small wedding and had expended a great deal of time and energy trying to come up with an arrangement that would allow all of our friends and family to attend. But nothing that we came up with worked for everyone involved, and, initially, we decided to postpone our wedding until the next year.

But now that we'd found each other, now that we knew we wanted to be together forever, we didn't want to wait any longer. We wanted to be married, we wanted to have children, and we wanted the rest of our lives to start *now.* "I won't regret not having a big wedding," Chad said, "but I'll regret waiting another year to start our family, and I'll regret celebrating our second wedding anniversary when we could be celebrating our third." I agreed with all of my heart. We decided to elope.

After that, everything else fell into place. We quickly settled on a location in Maui—a hotel in a remote, beautiful part of the island. I found the perfect wedding dress, but it was a few sizes too big, so I spent my evenings with a needle and thread, carefully altering the delicate lace by hand, pinning and tucking and stitching until it fit just right. When my dress was ready, I moved on to our wedding rings, making sure they were resized and ready for our trip. Then there was the actual business of getting married: the marriage license, booking the venue, going over our vows, and planning our trip to Hawaii.

Outside of work, our wedding was all I could think about, dream about, and write about. In the weeks leading up to our wedding day, I was full of excitement. "I did it. I found my soulmate. And, in seventeen days, I'm going to be his wife," I wrote in my journal, my heart filled with happiness and joy. It hardly seemed real to me. Somehow, I'd found the most incredible human being on this planet, I'd fallen in love with him, and he'd fallen in love with me, too. What we had was so much more than what could be encompassed by the word "love": We were each other's closest friend and confidant; we were partners in everything; we were so perfectly matched, our skills and strengths and weaknesses complementing each other. What we had was what I'd always dreamed of having, what I'd been holding out for, what I'd tried to convince everyone else was possible.

Our wedding was like a dream. It was the most wonderful, joyful day of my life.

We took a few days off work and planned to take a honeymoon later in the year, when things weren't quite so busy. When we returned home, we jumped right back into our work. In the week that followed, as I rode BART to and from Stripe's office next to AT&T Park, I read Viktor Frankl's *Man's Search for Meaning*. In Frankl's retelling of his horrific experiences in concentration camps during the Holocaust, he explained how the truth of one's character always comes out in the most difficult circumstances: "The way in which a man accepts his fate and all the suffering it entails, the way in which he takes up his cross, gives him ample opportunity—even under the most difficult circumstances—to add a deeper meaning to his life. . . . Here lies the chance for a man either to make use of or to forgo the opportunities of attaining the moral values that a difficult situation may afford him. And this decides whether he is worthy of his sufferings or not." As I read these words, I found myself judging my own fear, my inaction. I didn't need to be in the worst of circumstances to know my true character. No, my character was shining through at that very moment, and I didn't like what I saw: a person who lacked courage, who had a chance to stand up and do what was right but was too afraid to do it, who had escaped an awful situation and had done nothing to help those who were left behind. I had the morbid realization that if another one of my friends or former coworkers took their life and I had done and said nothing to prevent it, I would have blood on my hands.

I couldn't wait any longer. I'd already waited too long.

One Sunday morning, only a week after my wedding, I found myself sitting at my kitchen table, wrapped in my favorite blanket, my laptop open, my mind racing. I'd been trying to edit a few pages of a physics book I was writing, but had to give up. I couldn't stop thinking about what I'd experienced at Uber, what my friends were still going through, and my own cowardice. I checked my phone, hoping there might be a text from Chad saying he was coming home early from the gym or a text from my little sister about how her job was going, but there was nothing. I tried to watch an episode of *Seinfeld*, hoping it would distract me, but even that didn't work. I had to tell my story, and I had to do it *right now*.

I pulled up my blog and stared at the blank page in front of me.

I closed my laptop.

I thought about all of the ways this could go wrong, a thousand awful scenarios playing out in my head. If I came forward, I was certain that what happened to other whistleblowers and women who spoke out against sexual harassment and mistreatment would happen to me: I would lose my job, my reputation would be ruined, I would forever be branded "that woman who was sexually harassed," I would lose my friends, and—only one week into our marriage—there was a chance I would put my new husband and his company in jeopardy or in danger. And Uber wasn't just any old company: it was the most valuable private startup in Silicon

Valley history, and it played dirty; it played to win. I knew what it had done to journalists and to other employees: it had threatened the journalist Sarah Lacy and her family; it had sent a private investigator after ex-employee Morgan Richardson. Uber would come after me if I wrote something; of that, I was certain.

Based on everything I knew, sharing my story with the world would likely ruin my life. Sitting there, I couldn't help but think that after all I'd been through and everything I'd fought to accomplish, throwing it all away would be a colossal mistake. But there were no alternatives—none, at least, that seemed viable. No journalist was going to publish my story, and having agreed to mandatory arbitration as a condition of my employment, I couldn't publicly sue. There was, I thought to myself, a chance that I could have the arbitration clause thrown out by a judge, but the case would still likely be settled before it ever made it to court. Even if it did make it to trial, it would be too late by then—far too late—to help the people I'd left behind. No, going to a lawyer wouldn't solve anything. *Besides*, I thought, looking back on how I'd been advised when everything happened at Penn, *any lawyer worth her fee will tell me not to write a thing.*

I didn't know what to do. I felt, deep in my heart, that writing my story and sharing it with the world was the right thing to do, but the possible consequences were so awful that I couldn't believe it was something I was *actually* morally obligated to do. On the other hand, the price of doing nothing seemed just as great, if not far greater, than the cost of doing something; I feared that Uber would drive another employee to suicide.

In that moment, my mind led me back to a place I'd often

found myself before, trying to decide if moral obligation lay in the consequences of an action, in the action itself, or in the motive for the action. Was the right thing to do the thing that brought about the best consequences? Was it the thing that exemplified virtues like justice, honesty, and courage? Or was it something else? As I sat there in front of my laptop, I asked myself these questions over and over, hoping that the right answer would become obvious the more that I thought about it. I wanted to do what was right, and not just what was right for me, but what was *objectively* right.

And then it hit me: I had no way of possibly knowing what the consequences of my actions would be. I had no idea what would *actually* happen if I wrote the blog; I could only guess what would happen. But what if my guess was wrong? What if I was wrong about the consequences? Because I didn't have enough information to know what the consequences would be, I also couldn't know what the objectively right thing was to do. I could only have a subjective idea of what I should do, could only know what was the right thing to do given my extremely limited information. *And how on earth*, I thought, *could moral obligation really be determined by what brings about the best consequences, if you could never know what the consequences would be?*

To hell with the consequences, I decided. I had to put them aside and refuse to let them factor into my decision at all, so I thought about each painful possible consequence—my career being ruined, and nobody wanting to hire me; being branded a troublemaker or liability, as I'd been at Penn; having to start my life all over again, after I'd just finally begun a new career; being dragged into legal battles with Uber—and I let each one go. When the time came, I'd deal with the consequences, whatever they might be.

And in that moment, I knew what I was supposed to do. I realized that I'd been practicing for this day, for this decision, for many years. All of those years I'd journaled about myself and my life, trying to figure out who I was and trying to figure out how I could be better; all of those times that I'd sat down at my desk and reflected on my character, holding myself accountable, trying to develop virtues and avoid vices—that work had not only improved my character, and made me into a better person, but prepared me for *this*. I knew what was just, I knew what was truthful, I knew what was courageous, I knew what was right. Standing up against injustice was right. Refusing to give in to fear was right. Telling the truth was right. These things were right in every circumstance, regardless of the consequences.

I knew what I had to do. I had to speak up.

Now that I'd decided to write something, I thought very carefully about how to craft it. I couldn't show any emotion: my tone had to be measured, balanced, detached. I had to be careful with what I included in the post and deliberate in what I left out. I wouldn't name *anyone* in the post except by informal titles. And, critically, every single sentence I wrote had to be something I could back up with extensive written documentation.

I wrote the entire blog post, from start to finish, in less than an hour. Every word was deliberate, every sentence cautiously, purposefully composed. I wrote about Jake's messages and my interactions with HR; I wrote about my performance review being changed so I couldn't transfer; I wrote about the jackets and about my meeting with the CTO. Then I went into my office and hunted down every piece of physical documentation I had from my time at Uber, to make sure I could back up every single thing that I said: copies of the chat messages from Jake, printouts of my performance reviews, the email I'd sent to the head of HR about my conversation with Jan, and more. I combed through screenshots, photos, emails, journal entries, my personal calendar, and Post-it notes until I found every last piece I needed. Then I sat back and read through it one last time.

I pressed "publish."

CHAPTER ELEVEN

My blog post was picked up by almost every major media outlet within half an hour, and those first thirty minutes were the calm before the storm. Right after I'd published the blog post, I shared a link to it on Twitter. I watched as it was retweeted and shared by my friends, by their friends, by executives and investors in the tech community, by reporters, by celebrities. Then, like a flash flood, everything came pouring in. There was a flurry of text messages and phone calls—some from friends and family, others from unknown numbers—and notifications from social media. My Gmail and Twitter apps were the first to crash; I was receiving too many emails and tweets for them to keep up. My phone screen started flashing, unable to withstand the barrage of notifications, and my phone crashed, over and over. It would buzz as notifications flashed across the screen, then crash, power down, restart, and begin to buzz again. I felt paralyzed. With my phone rendered useless, I couldn't talk to anyone; I couldn't call Chad to warn him, couldn't

call my mother and stepfather to let them know that I was about
to be on the news.

I carefully picked up my endlessly crashing, buzzing, ringing,
restarting phone and carried it downstairs to the bedroom. I sat
on the floor beside the bed, put my phone on the ground, and
watched it buzz, ring, crash, and restart itself, over and over again.
I don't know how long I sat there, watching it, my mind unable to
fully comprehend what I'd just done. At some point, Chad came
home from the gym and found me sitting there on the floor, staring at my phone. Concerned, he asked what was going on. "Baby,"
I said, "I think I did something crazy."

For the rest of the day, Chad and I sat on our couch together
and watched as news outlets reported on my story. The press was
trying very hard to get in touch with me. My email inbox was
filled with requests from television stations, magazines, and news-
papers around the world. It took me a few hours to turn off the
notifications on my phone and stop it from crashing, and when I
did, I found my voicemail was full. Once he was able to get through
to me, my stepfather called, frantic and afraid, and told me that
he'd gotten a call from a producer at NBC News, who told him
that I was in an emergency and that NBC News needed to contact
me immediately; thinking that I had been hurt or was in trouble,
he'd given them my phone number. Many of my friends and relatives texted me, confused, because reporters were calling them
and asking for information about me and what I'd written.

It didn't take long for Uber to discover what I'd done. Several
hours after the post went live, Travis Kalanick retweeted it, saying,
"What's described here is abhorrent & against everything we

believe in. Anyone who behaves this way or thinks this is OK will be fired." A number of my friends and former coworkers from Uber contacted me. The ones who had experienced mistreatment, who knew what was going on at the company, weren't surprised by what I'd written and thanked me for speaking out. "Finally!" one friend said. A few Uber employees who I didn't know reached out and expressed shock and disbelief that such things had been happening at the company; some of them were angry at Uber, but quite a few of them were angry at me.

It wasn't long before I heard from my new employer. While the CEO and my direct manager commended me for my bravery, Stripe's head of communications did not seem happy. In a phone call that afternoon, she asked me why I hadn't gotten her approval before writing my post, and told me that I should get approval for anything else I said in the future. I assured her that I didn't plan on saying anything else—that I had no plans to speak to the press, to do any interviews, to go on national television. Relieved, she told me that was for the best, because, she said, "you don't want your name to be associated with sexual harassment, and neither does Stripe." She asked me to work from home until the press attention died down, because, she said, members of the press were going to come to the office looking for me.

I felt overwhelmed. To get out of the house and distract myself, I walked to the nearest bookstore, a Barnes & Noble, leaving my phone behind. I got a cup of coffee at the Starbucks inside, then meandered through the aisles of books and thought back to my childhood. Every Sunday afternoon after church, the Fowler family would pile into the old blue minivan that didn't have any air-conditioning and drive down to Phoenix. We'd stop at all the bookstores on Bell Road: first at the Borders, which had the best philosophy section, and then at the Barnes & Noble, which had the best fiction collection. We'd all spread out across the stores, each of us going to our favorite sections, and we'd sit in the aisles and read for hours. At that moment, I wished that my life could be that simple again. I picked up a biography of Abraham Lincoln and found a quiet place to sit in the computer science section. A few minutes later, I overheard two people in the aisle talking about my blog post, arguing about whether I was telling the truth and wondering about what would happen to Uber. I tried to ignore them but couldn't, so I decided to buy the biography and go home. When the cashier rang me up, she asked me, "So what did you do today?"

The truth was, I couldn't believe what I'd done that day. I knew that writing the blog post was the right thing to do, and I knew that *someone* would read it, that it would get some attention from the press and the public, but I had no idea just how many people would read my story. Before I left the house, I'd checked the site traffic; I expected hundreds of visits, maybe a few thousand. The most visitors any of my blog posts had received was around a hundred thousand, for a post I wrote about learning physics. But when I saw the numbers, I couldn't believe my eyes: millions upon millions of people had read my blog in the first six hours. *Millions.* I'd been afraid of the consequences before, but now I was terrified.

As I walked home, I kept thinking about what Stripe's head of communications had told me over the phone: "You don't want your name to be associated with sexual harassment." Her words played on repeat in my head. *This is what everyone will know me for, for the rest of my life*, I thought. *I'll always be the woman who was sexually harassed at Uber.* I thought of all the things I had done in my life, all of the struggles I'd fought through and everything I'd accomplished. I had pulled my way out of poverty, educated myself, gotten myself into one of the best schools in the world, learned physics, taught myself software engineering, published a book on software architecture. Those challenges had seemed insurmountable at the time, but, in retrospect, they hadn't been the hardest parts of my life—what had been impossible to overcome were the obstacles that other people had thrown in my path. Making myself the hero of my story when other people were hell-bent on making me the victim—becoming the subject, rather than the object, of my life—those were the battles I could never figure out how to win. Time and time again, when I was fighting for my education and for fair treatment from my employers, at ASU, and at Penn, I had ultimately lost. In the end, the institutions were stronger and more powerful than I was, and they'd always had something I desperately wanted, something they could hold over my head, something they could take away. Until today.

I realized that every one of those experiences had prepared me for what was happening now. It wasn't the most comforting thought; if I could have, I would have chosen to erase all of those painful moments from my life; I would have given anything to have lived a life in which I'd been free to be myself, free to chase and accomplish my dreams without fear of retribution. But now there was a possibility that none of those awful situations had been in vain: I'd learned from them, and maybe, just maybe, I'd finally found a way to become the protagonist of my own story. Maybe, I thought, people will think of me not as "the woman who was harassed at Uber" but as "the woman who stood up and spoke out about harassment at Uber."

When I returned home that night, along with all the shock and numbness and distance from my body I'd been feeling since the blog post had gone viral that morning, I felt peace in my heart. Yes, perhaps people would only ever know me for this blog post— but was that really such a terrible fate? That would mean they knew me because I had done something important, because I had stood up for myself and shared my story. And maybe, just maybe, reading my story would give them the courage to do the same.

I woke up early the next morning, relieved that yesterday had passed, and started my day as if nothing had happened. I walked upstairs to the kitchen, where Chad was making a pot of pour-over coffee and one of his favorite blueberry-banana-coconut milk smoothies. I gave him a kiss, popped a pretzel bagel in the toaster, and sat down at the table with my laptop. I was certain that, like most viral news stories, my blog post would soon be forgotten. When I opened my email and looked at my Twitter feed, I discovered that people seemed more interested in my story today than they'd been the day before. I closed my personal laptop and put it aside, then pulled out my Stripe laptop and tried to put all of my attention into working on the upcoming issue of *Increment*.

The events of the first few days after the blog post were more of the same. Every morning, I'd wake up and spend a little time with Chad over breakfast before he went to work. Then I would take a shower, get dressed, and start to pack up my things for work before remembering that the press was probably still waiting for me at the Stripe office and that I was supposed to work from home. I'd pull my laptop out of my backpack, walk into my little office, sit at my desk, and work until the end of the day. Sitting in front of my laptop, I'd try to keep my focus on my work, but my mind was always torn in another direction. With new emails piling up in my inbox every hour, and calls and texts interrupting me every few minutes, I couldn't help but feel anxious and distracted.

To make matters worse, there was a brand-new story in the papers about me or Uber every single day. I was able to push aside the small stories, but the bigger ones were impossible to ignore. The day after my blog post, Travis Kalanick and Uber hired Eric Holder, the former U.S. attorney general under President Obama, and Tammy Albarrán, a partner at the law firm Covington & Burling, to "conduct an independent review into the specific issues relating to the work place environment raised by Susan Fowler, as well as diversity and inclusion at Uber more broadly." The investigation, Uber announced, would be overseen by Arianna Huffington and Uber's chief HR officer, Liane Hornsey.

But the message Kalanick wanted to send—that Uber was a responsible company that was taking this seriously—was soon eclipsed by a long exposé in *The New York Times*, in which reporter Mike Isaac detailed Uber's toxic, "Hobbesian" culture, covering everything from a manager's assaulting an employee with a baseball bat to the harassment, assault, theft, and drug use that had occurred during the infamous "Vegas trip" that had delayed my on-site interview at Uber. In the wake of this report, two of Uber's earliest investors—Mitch Kapor and Freada Kapor Klein— penned an open letter to Uber's board and investors that was picked up by multiple media outlets; in the letter, they said that they had known about Uber's culture for a long time and had been trying to quietly change it from the inside. Waymo, a Google subsidiary that was developing self-driving cars, sued Uber for patent infringement and trade secret theft, and a video leaked of Travis Kalanick berating an Uber driver.

There was something validating about all the stories that were finally coming out about problems at Uber, because they proved to the world that my mistreatment and the mistreatment of my colleagues weren't isolated incidents and that, as I knew all too well, Uber's mistreatment of employees and egregious corporate behavior weren't limited to sexual harassment. But it was more exhausting and frustrating than validating: I couldn't wrap my head around the fact that so many powerful people inside the company—like some of its investors and high-ranking employees—had known about how terrible Uber's culture was, yet none of them had taken their stories to the public until I had. It was one thing for people *outside* Uber to criticize it—and many people had, criticizing it for the way it paid and treated drivers and for the way it subverted or flat-out ignored regulations—but it was an entirely different thing for people inside Uber, who knew about the emotional and physical abuse of employees, who knew that employees were pushed to their breaking points, to know and to say nothing. Reading things like the Kapors' letter, I felt angry: the company's investors had known *this whole time*, and they had done nothing.

Meanwhile, emails, messages, comments, and tweets were pouring in from people who expressed every manner of opinion about what I'd done. People from across the world and from all walks of life thanked me for coming forward. Other women who had been public victims of harassment and discrimination, like Gretchen Carlson, sent me messages of support and encouragement. Celebrities and politicians sent me kind messages, and even spoke up in support of me at public events; Hillary Clinton, in her first official speaking appearance since the election, mentioned my blog post and publicly supported me. Of course, there were messages of hate, too. "We need to see if it is really sexism or feminist delusion," one commenter wrote on my blog. "Here say [*sic*]. Libel," another person wrote. "Hope you don't have any traceable deposits from Lyft or you may end up in prison." The comments didn't stop: "You play the victim card very well"; "Boo Fucking Hoo . . . I call bullshit"; "Shut the fuck up and get on with your life, nobody cares about your psycho drama."

The majority of the emails and messages I received, however, were from thousands of people who wanted to share their stories of harassment, discrimination, and retaliation. Some of them had worked in academia and had been forced out of their tenure-track and tenured jobs because they had been harassed or discriminated against. Others had been forced into arbitration, secret settlements, or gag orders by companies where they had experienced every form of discrimination and retaliation you can imagine. Many of the things these people had endured were far worse than anything I had experienced or seen. They had been assaulted at work, stalked by coworkers and bosses, fired for being pregnant, spoken to in the worst and most insulting ways. Many of them said that they wished they had gone public, but that they had been too scared. My blog post had changed the world, some said: for the first time, a woman had spoken up about mistreatment, the world listened to her, and she walked away unscathed.

And, in those early days, it really did seem that I had turned the tables, that—aside from the hateful comments online and having to work from home for a while—there was a chance I might emerge without having suffered any of the typical consequences for whistleblowing. I started to wonder if most of my fears—about Uber coming after me, about people trying to discredit me, about my career and future being in jeopardy—had been unfounded. It seemed too good to be true.

And it was. I was soon jolted out of my daydream, and I awakened to a nightmare.

CHAPTER **TWELVE**

Not long after the blog post went live, I began to hear strange stories from my family, friends, and acquaintances. Reporters had been contacting them from day one and asking for information about me—which was annoying, but to be expected—but now they were also being contacted by people who didn't seem to be reporters at all. Again and again, I heard the same type of story: a friend or family member was contacted by someone who asked for "personal" information about me, posing open-ended questions that didn't seem right—questions about my personal life, questions about my past. Some of these strange people were calling from unlisted numbers and identified themselves using names and titles that, according to Google searches, appeared to be fake. The frequency of these strange interactions increased with every passing day.

Some friends let me know that they'd been contacted, but assured me they didn't say anything. Others admitted that they might have said too much. And there were still others who I knew had been contacted but who said nothing to me, which scared me most of all.

Initially, it was mostly my relatives and friends from Silicon Valley who were being contacted, but then they—whoever "they" were—began contacting people I hadn't spoken to in years. Whoever was trying to dig up dirt on me was going deep into my history, talking to people that I'd forgotten I'd even known. I didn't know who was trying to get this information, and I didn't know how they were able to find out so much about my past. I didn't know what they were looking for, and I didn't know what they were going to find. It was terrifying.

One of the people they located was a classmate from community college whom I hadn't spoken to since 2006. Another was an old next-door neighbor whom I hadn't seen since I was a young teenager. "Someone's digging really deep on you, Susan," my old neighbor said, "and it's scary how far back they're going." They contacted a professor who had written one of my letters of recommendation for college. When he contacted me, he was panicked and scared on my behalf; there was no way anyone could know that we knew each other unless they had seen my college application information. Overwhelmed and frightened, I put off calling some of my old friends after they had first alerted me to the situation, including the old professor. When I finally tried to contact him, I found out that he had died. It was awful, knowing that the man who had played the biggest role in getting me into college, who had mentored me and done everything in his power to help me build a better life for myself, was gone, and that the last conversation he ever had about me was with a private investigator.

Eventually, private investigators began contacting me directly. It was a surreal experience. I'd already been contacted by hundreds of reporters, who would (almost) always identify themselves and try to persuade me to talk on the record (which I refused to do). Most of the time, it was easy to verify that the reporters were who they said they were: I could contact their editors and ask them to confirm the reporters' contact information; I could look at their social media profiles and confirm that they were real; I could read the things they had written in the past. But every once in a while, I'd get calls from people who weren't who they said they were; either their information couldn't be verified, or a Google search indicated that nobody with their name or title worked where they said they were employed. The experiences were eerily similar to what some of my friends had described: a person reached out, using a spoofed or blocked number, using a name that wasn't real, asking questions about things in ways that most reporters would never ask. I rarely answered my phone, only ever picking it up if the call came from a number I recognized or if I was expecting a call from someone at that exact time.

Once, when I was waiting for a furniture delivery and expecting the furniture company to call me, I received a call from a number I didn't recognize, and answered. A woman was on the line, gave me her name, identified herself as a private investigator, claimed that she was working on a case *against* Uber, and asked me to help her. I declined with a laugh, then did some detective work on my own, only to find that the PI firm that she worked for dealt almost exclusively with cases in which it helped companies who were trying to discredit victims of sexual harassment and sexual assault.

Meanwhile, someone was also trying to get into my social media accounts. My phone would "ding" whenever I received a two-factor authentication text belonging to my email account, my Facebook account, or my Twitter account, which meant that someone was trying to hack into my accounts. I reset my passwords. I changed my passwords frequently, and even got a second phone for 2FA texts, but it wasn't enough. My Facebook account was hacked several times, as were several old email accounts I hadn't used in years. Around the same time, my younger sister's Facebook account was hacked using a popular phishing technique. The moment she told me that someone else had gotten into her account, I logged in and looked at the messages I'd recently sent her. I watched as they went from "unread" to "read."

A deep, aching terror fell like a shadow over me as I prepared for the worst parts of my life to become public. Meanwhile, I was growing increasingly isolated—I was still working from home, and there were very few people I could talk to about the things that were happening; more than once, I confided in a friend, only to have our conversation parroted back to me by a reporter a few days later. I felt sick to my stomach every day and had trouble sleeping. I'd lie awake in the middle of the night, trying not to wake my husband, racking my brain for memories of every mean thing I'd ever said, every mistake I'd ever made, every wrong thing I'd ever done, every lie I'd ever told, every person I'd ever hurt. I was haunted by every fight, every angry text message, every mean word, every breakup. I went over and over in my head everything I'd said that could be misinterpreted, that could put me in a bad light; every joke I'd ever told that might offend someone else;

every stupid or wrong thing I'd ever believed and possibly repeated. I thought of all the ways that the facts of my life could be twisted and used to hurt me, of how easy it would be for Uber to discredit me using something like my stay at the mental health facility after my father died. Just like every other person on this earth, I had made countless mistakes and had done a million things that I could very easily be publicly crucified for, and I was sure that whoever was after me would try to find a way to use that information to discredit and destroy me.

I didn't know who or what I was up against. I was certain it was Uber, though I had no concrete evidence to back that up. Several security researchers offered to look into it, and came back with the names of various private investigation firms that Uber had hired in the past, including the one that had tried to break into Morgan Richardson's house the previous year. Its most recent PI firm, I was told, was an opposition research company run by former CIA operatives. This terrified me even more.

I begged Uber to stop. I sent emails to Uber's executives and board members, asking them to call off their investigators or, if they weren't the ones behind it, to publicly state that they weren't and denounce whoever was. Arianna Huffington, the board member overseeing Holder's investigation, replied, saying that she didn't think it was Uber. She said she had asked the executive team and they told her that they hadn't ordered it, but they wouldn't publicly deny or denounce it. Though inside Uber she claimed that she and I were talking regularly, and she went on the news and said that she and I were "emailing regularly," that was the first and only time I ever engaged with her.

In desperation, I tweeted that I suspected I was the target of a smear campaign. This finally caught Uber's attention. Uber was adamant that the company wasn't behind it. They stated publicly that they weren't running any separate investigations on me; the only lawyers they had hired to look into my allegations, they said, were Eric Holder and Tammy Albarrán.

I was relieved, and for the first time in what felt like a very long time, I felt like I could breathe again. But my relief was short-lived: I soon discovered that they had lied, when, one night, I received an email from another lawyer Uber had hired, who admitted she was running a separate, independent investigation into me.

While I waited fearfully for whatever they were digging up about my past to come to light, the rumors about me and my motivations were already swirling, and I soon got the sense that they were coming from within Uber's walls. The first rumor I'd heard had come from a reporter who called me in late February to see if I could confirm something she had heard from a source: that Lyft had paid me to write a defamatory blog post about Uber. It was obviously false, and I told her so. Within a few days, I heard versions of the same rumor from other reporters, from people in the tech industry, and from employees at Uber, all centered on Lyft's paying me to write the blog post.

As soon as this rumor died down, another one quickly took its place: that powerful venture capitalists in Silicon Valley had been responsible for writing the blog post and making it go viral; in some versions of this rumor, those "powerful people" were investors in Lyft, Google, or Chad's company. A reporter from *Business Insider* wrote in an email (which I never responded to) that she was writing about a "conspiracy theory that someone related to your husband's company encouraged you to write the post and then helped it go viral after you wrote it."

When those rumors didn't stick, new rumors came out—some attacking my character, others that seemed to call my motives into question. I had done it for fame; it was a publicity stunt; I was writing a book about Uber and trying to drum up press for it (I didn't obtain a book contract until much, much later). Some of the rumors crossed over into the absurd: that my husband had "secretly" been a manager at Uber when we met, and that to cover up our relationship I had lied about the sexual harassment from Jake; that Uber executives were partaking in regular orgies and that young women engineers, including me, were part of them; and that I was a terrible writer and my husband must have written the blog post for me.

I was pretty sure that many of these rumors were being spread by Uber, because my friends who were still there told me that they were being circulated within the company. One friend was in the women's bathroom when she overheard a female manager quietly tell two other female employees that they shouldn't believe what I had written, because I was being paid by their competitors to spread lies. Another friend was told by a manager that I was being blackmailed by Lyft investors. In addition, many of the rumors I heard from reporters and others outside Uber were always accompanied by phrases like "someone close to Uber," "someone close to the board," or even "someone *at* Uber."

I wanted to go on the record to all the reporters who contacted me and tell them some of the things I was experiencing, from the private investigators to the hacked accounts. Instead, I kept a low profile, only confirming or denying things off the record in the most serious cases. I knew I had to stay quiet. I might have won the battle, but I hadn't yet won the war. As it stood, the things I'd written in my post were just allegations—damning allegations, but allegations nonetheless. Yes, some of the reporting about Uber that had come out in the wake of the post had backed up a handful of my claims about the company's culture, but that wasn't enough. Any justice that came out of the public response to my post was nothing more than mob justice, and that wasn't enough for me or for anyone else who truly cared about the issues and wanted real, lasting change. Because I couldn't publicly sue Uber, my only hope was that an independent investigation would substantiate my claims. Eric Holder's investigation still had a long way to go, and until he released his report, I would have to sit and wait it out.

The only outlet I had to address gossip and rumors or share updates was Twitter. I tried not to tweet very often, but if there was something that I absolutely needed to address, Twitter was the easiest and most effective way to do it. Anytime I tweeted about Uber or anything related to Uber, it was picked up by reporters and found its way into that day's news. Uber hated when I tweeted, and was angry every time I did. At one point, Eric Holder himself asked me to stop tweeting and told me it was best that I remain quiet until after the investigation had ended. To make matters worse, Stripe was also unhappy with the press attention around my blog post, and its head of communications wanted me to sign a formal agreement stating that I would not say anything publicly without the company's approval; she said that I was bringing too much attention to Stripe, and that reporters were calling her and asking her about Stripe's culture. I refused to sign the agreement but promised Stripe I wouldn't say anything that might bring negative attention to the company. Afraid of angering Eric Holder and jeopardizing the investigation, certain that I would lose my job if I said anything more, I fell silent.

As terrifying and infuriating as the investigations and rumors were, nothing was as scary as being followed, which started happening shortly after I published the post.

At Stripe's request, I worked from home for the rest of February and into the first weeks of March; when I eventually returned to the office, I was told that there were still people waiting outside the office to talk to me, so I used a side door to enter and exit the building. I noticed a peculiar car parked outside my house. When I walked from my house to the BART station on my way to the office, I'd often see the same car drive past me. (*Or is it really the same one?* I would wonder.) Whenever I left the office, I couldn't shake the feeling that I was being followed. I told myself that I was imagining it.

Then, one afternoon in early March, I left the office earlier than usual. As I walked down the back steps of the office and turned the corner toward the street, I noticed a man jump—as if in surprise—and start walking after me. I changed directions as I walked, going down side streets that I normally never traveled, and whenever I glanced back, I saw him following a short distance behind. I eventually ducked into the Whole Foods on Fourth and Harrison, and watched as he walked past me. I let out a sigh of relief and told myself that I was just being paranoid, that there was nobody following me. I walked back out into the street, only to see the man standing several dozen feet ahead of me, leaning on a tree, looking down at the sidewalk. I quickly walked past him, and he followed closely, steadily behind. I walked up the steps of a large building, and as he came closer, I stopped and stepped down toward the street. He walked past me, then stopped, turned around, and looked right at me. I felt the panic rise in my throat, felt my heart beating so loudly I could hear it even over the chaos of the street. I looked around for the police, hoping to find someone, anyone, who could help me. I wanted to shout, but we were in the middle of the city, surrounded by people, and I was afraid that everyone would think I was crazy if I started screaming that I was being followed. Not knowing what to do, I bolted as fast as I could down the street, down into the BART station, and onto a train.

That was the first time that I knew I was definitely being followed, and it wasn't the last. I was followed and stalked by private investigators up until the writing of this book.

It's difficult to put into words how all of this felt. How it felt when friends told me they might have said too much to a private investigator. How it felt to read emails from reporters asking me to comment on something disparaging about myself or my husband that wasn't true, and not being able to say anything because I didn't want to be fired or jeopardize the investigation. How it felt to be followed everywhere I went. How it felt to live in constant fear. It was hell. I felt like I had died and the sum of my life was being examined by a judge who knew only every stupid or foolish or wrong thing that I had ever done and every rumor that had ever been spread about me, and refused to take into account any of the good or the truth. But I couldn't see the judge, couldn't see who was trying to destroy me, didn't know what they were going to use to bring me down; I was blindfolded, my hands were tied, I couldn't even make my own case, and most of the things used against me were baseless rumors and lies. Some days, the anxiety, fear, and horror of it got so bad that I would curl up into a ball on the floor and cry until I felt numb. On the worst days, I would stand in the shower, turn on the water, cover my mouth with my hands, and scream into my hands until my voice was hoarse. Part of what felt so scary was the randomness of it all: I never knew what to expect.

But later that spring, I met Sarah Lacy, the journalist who had been the target of an Uber smear campaign a few years earlier. We met for drinks in a small, quiet bar in San Francisco's Mission District, and she told me what Uber had done to her—the way its executives had publicly threatened her and her family, the things that they'd discovered about her through their investigations that they tried to use against her—and I shared the strange and distressing experiences I'd had. It was surreal: I would be describing something that had happened, like seeing a strange car following me, and she would be able to finish the story because she had experienced the exact same thing; she could even describe *exactly* what the car looked like.

I confessed to her that it was hard for me to talk to other

people about this, because it made me feel like I was losing my mind. This was not the stuff of real life but the stuff you see in movies, and it couldn't possibly be happening to me.

"But it *is* happening to me," I said. "And I feel like I'm going fucking crazy."

She grabbed my hands. "You are not crazy," she said, looking me in the eye. "Do you hear me? You are not crazy."

Then she introduced me to what she called the "opposition playbook," the strategy that some companies used whenever you made them look bad. First, they hired opposition researchers and private investigators to dig into your past, calling up people you hadn't spoken to in years, trying to find something—anything—they could use against you. Second, they'd watch you and follow you, trying to catch you doing things that made you look bad, like talking to their competitors or talking to reporters. Third, they'd sow seeds of doubt in the public, which would start out as innocent-sounding comments on social media (from fake accounts) that took something innocuous you'd said and twisted it into something horrible; then they'd straight up say defamatory things about you and try to persuade people to doubt what you'd said. I was dumbfounded. Everything that had been happening to me since I published the blog post now made sense.

Still, I couldn't sleep at night. I was terrified that Uber would send a private investigator to break into our home, either while we were there or while we were out. If they did it to Morgan Richardson, what was stopping them from doing it to me? What if, I wondered, they had already done it and we just didn't know? Chad and I had private security guard us and watch our apartment while we slept.

I was warned by a few of my friends that if Uber didn't already have my medical records, they would probably get their hands on them soon, and that there was a chance they would use them to discredit me. This was a very real fear for me, and something I'd experienced before: during my last year at Penn, school administrators acquired my medical records as part of their investigation. I never found out if Uber got my medical records, but, a few months later, news came out that they'd illegally acquired the medical records of a woman who had been raped in an Uber, and they'd tried to use her records to discredit her.

Several people warned me that my life was in danger. "I wouldn't be surprised if they have you killed," one famous person in the tech industry said. Tens of billions of dollars were at stake. I'd never been one to scare easily, but I was terrified. I was terrified for my life, for my husband, for my family, for my friends and former coworkers still at Uber. One morbid thought gave me comfort, however, and it's what I told myself every time I noticed someone following me, or whenever I was warned about possible threats against my life: if anything happened to me, if I was harmed or killed, everyone would know exactly who was responsible.

I wasn't the only one going through hell. At the same time, some Uber employees were going through similar things—being contacted by strange people, being followed by private investigators, receiving friend requests from fake social media accounts, being gaslighted by Uber.

The investigation into Uber's culture was indeed underway,

and it was moving very quickly. But contrary to all of the messaging around the investigation that Uber shared with its customers and the press, there wasn't just one investigation in progress. There were three: the one being conducted by Eric Holder, another being conducted by the law firm Perkins Coie, and another involving Uber's own internal lawyers.

According to my friends who were still at the company, it seemed like the three investigations were racing to see who could dig up the documentation and interview everyone first. One friend of mine was told being interviewed was mandatory, but the lawyers interviewing him refused to tell him *which* investigation they belonged to. They asked him questions about me, my character, and what else I knew about but had left out of my blog post. Then, at the end, they said they were not part of Holder's investigation into Uber's culture, but Perkins Coie's investigation into me and my allegations. Another friend said that when she requested a lawyer be present in her interview with Uber's lawyers, they refused to allow it. Yet another friend told me that at the end of his interview one of the lawyers demanded to know what exactly Susan Fowler might be planning next.

If Uber employees declined to meet with the investigators or requested a lawyer, they were sternly reprimanded. One of the women from the LadyEng group showed me an email that she had received from Uber's legal team in which she and other employees were told that if they didn't meet with Uber's investigators, they would be fired. They were also told that they were not allowed to bring lawyers to these meetings; according to Uber's legal team, employees did not have the right to have a lawyer present because "this is not a police interrogation."

The chaos escalated rapidly. If Uber's internal lawyers got to something or someone first, they would destroy evidence and try to scare and intimidate employees. Several of the women who had made harassment and discrimination complaints during my time at Uber started to put their own documentation together to hand over to Holder's investigation, only to find that their emails, screenshots, and files about harassment and discrimination had been deleted from their email accounts. After one of my friends met with investigators, her personal phone and computer were stolen from her desk. When she reported the theft to Uber's security, they said that the office cameras normally watching her desk were turned off at the time, so they couldn't help her. Another friend had his personal phone stolen from his desk, in the exact same situation, several days later.

One night after I'd gone back to work at Stripe, Laura and I met for dinner in the city. We hadn't seen each other in months. When she walked into the restaurant and our eyes met, I almost burst into tears. She had been my closest friend at Uber, and I missed her terribly. We had been through so many horrible experiences together at Uber, and we were still going through the worst of it, with no end in sight.

We talked over pizza and wine. I told her how I was being followed, how Uber was digging deep into my past, contacting everyone I knew, how I was terrified and felt alone. Then she caught me up on what had been going on with her. Ever since I'd left, things had only gotten worse. Despite an excellent performance review, she was told she wasn't technical enough, and when she tried to transfer to another team, her request was blocked—the same way mine had been. Clearly, Thuan Pham hadn't followed through on his promise to end this practice. The mistreatment had only escalated from there. When the investigations first began, Uber employees were encouraged to speak to the new head of HR—Liane Hornsey, who'd joined right after I left—about mistreatment within the company, and Laura took them up on their offer. She went to Liane, to Arianna Huffington, and to other company executives, expecting that they would finally keep their word, that they would do something about it. But they did nothing. Eventually, Liane told Laura that they hadn't found any evidence of wrongdoing. Even when they were in the hot seat, with the whole world watching, Uber was still broken, unable to do the right thing.

CHAPTER **THIRTEEN**

When I heard that Uber was destroying documentation, I asked
Eric Holder to put a stop to it. As far as I know, he never placed a
documentation hold. We did, however, schedule a meeting.

I felt so nervous in the days leading up to our meeting. I didn't
know if Holder's intentions were good or bad; he was, after all,
working for Uber, and given that he didn't seem bothered by the
destruction of documentation material to his investigation, I
wasn't sure that I could trust him. And there was so much at stake.
I feared that if I said or did the wrong thing, if I contradicted
myself, or if I came across as dishonest or insincere, there was a
chance I would jeopardize the situation for everyone. I thought of
my friend Laura, and everything she had been through; of my
friends Ashley, Roxana, Eamon, and Rick; of Joseph Thomas,
Morgan Richardson, Sarah Lacy; of everyone at Uber who had
attempted or committed suicide, been bullied by their managers,
been lied to by HR. If Holder's investigation didn't substantiate
the things I'd written, not only would my reputation be destroyed,

but things at Uber would likely never get better because the company would never be forced to change.

I was so frustrated and angry that coming forward hadn't made things better for my friends and colleagues still at Uber. In fact, things had only gotten worse; in the months following the blog post, Uber's mistreatment of employees had grown even more absurd and awful. The company clearly wasn't going to change of its own accord, and our only hope was that Holder's investigation would publicly corroborate the allegations in my blog post and force Uber to take serious steps to reform. I knew, deep within my heart, that I had to overcome my fears and meet with Holder. I had to prove to him that what I'd said in my blog post was true, and I had to tell him about everything that had happened, about everything I'd left out.

And so, one day in April—only a few days before my twenty-sixth birthday—I met with Eric Holder and Tammy Albarrán.

I'd seen Holder on television so many times, and I almost couldn't believe I was really in the same room with him. He was unlike anyone I'd ever met before, more politician than lawyer. He talked to people as if they were his closest friends; his voice was warm and kind, and he joked in a relaxed way that made everyone in the room feel at ease.

The table between us was covered with tidily stacked binders filled with evidence: printed-out, carefully annotated copies of emails, legal documents, internal Uber company chats, photographs, handwritten notes, and, of course, my blog post. Many of the binders belonged to Holder and Albarrán, but one of them belonged to me. It was all there: the messages in which Jake had sexually harassed me, my performance reviews, the emails about the leather jackets, my resignation letter, the emails from Thuan acknowledging he was aware that managers had been blocking their female employees' transfers. It was all the documentation I had used to blow the whistle, that backed up every word of my blog post, that had the potential to set me and my coworkers free.

We sat around that table for several hours, Holder asking me questions about my blog post and my time at Uber and Albarrán grilling me on the details of each of my answers. Holder would approach things in a disarmingly warm and friendly manner, asking me to share my side of the story, nodding and smiling as I recounted my experiences. Then Albarrán would jump in, asking me for precise details about dates, times, names, the ordering of particular events. Sometimes, she would ask me to confirm or deny specific details that were, more often than not, incorrect. I tripped up a few times when she asked me to confirm incorrect details and had to catch myself and back up the conversation so that I could correct the information. At first, I couldn't tell if she was doing it on purpose, but it happened frequently enough that by the end of our meeting I was pretty certain she was.

The intense questioning was punctuated by casual conversation. Behind Holder and Albarrán, a wall of windows faced onto San Francisco Bay and Alcatraz Island. In between questions, I would stare out at the bay and that strange little island. These moments were brief; it was never long before the binders were flipped open again and the questioning resumed. At one point during our meeting, the pressure got to me. There was no way someone like me could go up in front of the former U.S. attorney general and succeed. I feared that if Holder was out to discredit me, there was nothing I could do. *I am not prepared for this*, I thought. *There is no way I could have prepared for this.* I had to take a break and walk around outside, down Market Street and then back up again, wringing my hands, trying to calm my mind and nerves.

Eventually, after several hours, we had covered it all—everything from my very first days at Uber to the destruction of documentation that was going on right under their noses.

"Do you have any further questions for me?" Holder asked, as everyone around the table closed up their binders and began to pack them away. I had a thousand questions I wanted to ask him, a thousand things I wanted to know. But I knew that if I asked him anything, there was a chance it might bias him and his investigation. The stakes were too high; the risks were too great. I kept my mouth shut.

"No," I answered, shaking my head.

In the weeks after my meeting with Holder and Albarrán, one by one my old friends from Uber stopped talking to me. One of them told me later that Uber had found out she was talking to me—even though we'd been careful to use end-to-end encryption and send messages that self-destructed—and she was afraid they were going to retaliate against her for it. I had difficulty connecting with many of my friends outside Uber, too. Shalon was one of the few people who understood, who didn't look at me like I was crazy when I tried to explain things that were going on, like being followed or having my social media accounts hacked.

In the loneliness of those days, I was fortunate to meet a number of people on the good side of the tech world. I met venture capitalists, tech company executives, and industry leaders who encouraged me, gave me advice, and even offered to pay for my legal fees (I politely declined, though I appreciated their kindness and generosity). I met other women who had gone through similar experiences, who had been the victims of harassment and discrimination, had gone public, and had lived to tell the tale. When they told me about their experiences and thanked me for speaking out, I felt a little less alone.

Chad was my foundation the entire time, supporting me and loving me through the worst of it all. Thanks to my blog post, we'd never had those wonderful honeymoon weeks that everyone told us were the best part of being newlyweds. Even so, somewhere in the hectic anxiety and terror of the past two months, we managed to find moments of peace and joy. We'd curl up on the couch at night and watch *Game of Thrones* or World War II movies, and crawl into bed next to each other and read together until we fell asleep. We'd take our long walks through the eucalyptus groves of Tilden Park and forget that the rest of the world existed. Somewhere in the sanctuary of those moments, we decided that we wouldn't let Uber—or anyone—steal away the joy and love we had in our life together, that we wouldn't let the public drama unfolding in our lives keep us from doing the things we had always dreamed of, like starting a family.

We began to settle into the rhythm of our new, very different life. I'd been hoping every day that the attention would stop and that life would return to normal. I wanted to be able to go to work without being followed by private investigators, without being recognized by strangers on BART. I wanted to be able to scroll through my Twitter and Facebook feeds without seeing strangers and reporters mentioning my name. I wanted to be able to say things on social media without Uber, Eric Holder, or Stripe immediately jumping on me, without it ending up in the news. But I knew that in the scheme of things, my problems were small. I was still alive; I was married to the man I loved; I still had a job, and it was a job that I loved. In fact, the first issue of *Increment* had just launched and was doing very well; the famed technology journalist Kara Swisher had called it *"The New Yorker* for geeks." And despite Uber's best efforts, I hadn't been crucified in the press.

The anxiety, the fear, and the background noise of terror were still there, but I'd grown accustomed to them. I found happiness in the realization that my life was finally converging toward the life I'd always wanted for myself: I was working full-time as a writer and editor—something I'd always dreamed of doing, but never thought I'd be able to achieve. I was married to a brilliant, loving, wonderful man. And, in May, I found out I was pregnant with our first child.

When I learned a month later that I was carrying a baby girl, I felt a renewed sense of urgency in making the world a better place. I didn't want my daughter to grow up in a world where sexual harassment, discrimination, and retaliation were commonplace. I wanted her to grow up in a world where the only things she had to worry about were whether her dreams were big enough and whether she was working hard enough to achieve them.

Every day, as I waited for Holder's report to arrive, I worked. Amid the never-ending attention of the public, the press, and Uber, I went into the Stripe office and worked with my team on issues of our new magazine, commissioning pieces for future issues, searching for a managing editor, combing over print proofs, and editing pieces. When I came home from work, I'd walk up the stairs of our apartment to my tiny office, where I did my best to shut out the world. I'd turn off the internet on my laptop and my phone and work on the science-fiction novel I'd been writing. I'd play my violin softly and sing to the tiny baby girl growing inside me. When Chad came home, I'd hold him close. I cherished these moments of peace, when it was just me, my own work, my baby, and my husband. Whenever I turned my phone back on, the chaos returned, my email inbox full again, another string of expletives and threats in my Twitter notifications, another group of messages from men and women all over the world, asking why there hadn't been any consequences for the perpetrators, asking whether there was any hope that things would truly change. I didn't know what to tell them. I didn't have any answers.

In those uncertain days, while we waited for Holder's investigation to conclude, I wondered if I had done enough, if I should have been more vocal, if I should have been louder, braver, stronger.

Meanwhile, the world was watching the Uber drama play out. It seemed like everyone was desperately hoping that the Holder report would confirm my blog post, that it would be a turning point not only for Uber, but for women in technology and in the workplace. I found solace in the fact that my blog post was already starting to make a difference in the world. After reading my story, other women in Silicon Valley were inspired to speak up about the mistreatment they'd experienced, and bravely went to the press with their stories. "Susan inspired us," said Leiti Hsu, who, along with five other women, shared her story of being sexually harassed by the venture capitalist Justin Caldbeck. As I read their stories and carefully watched the media reaction, I couldn't help but notice how different the response to their stories was in comparison with the stories from women who had spoken up in the past. They were being taken seriously, and, even more surprising, reporters wanted to write about their experiences. The world was beginning to change.

On June 13, Eric Holder delivered Covington & Burling's report to the board. The board released an abridged version to the public; the full report has, surprisingly, never been leaked to the press or to the public. The report went well beyond confirming the claims I'd made in my blog post, and painted a grim picture of the company: an organization so dysfunctional and broken that its culture needed to be completely torn down and rebuilt from scratch. The list of recommendations included things like ensuring the company had "appropriate tools, including complaint tracking software" to keep track of employee complaints; training for human resources personnel on how to effectively handle complaints; a policy banning romantic relationships between managers and their employees; and that Uber "reformulate its written cultural values," especially those that had been used "to justify poor behavior, including Let Builders Build, Always Be Hustlin', Meritocracy and Toe-Stepping, and Principled Confrontation." Answering the question of who was responsible for the broken culture at Uber, at the very top of the list was the most important recommendation of all: "Review and Reallocate the Responsibilities of Travis Kalanick." Immediately after the report was released, Kalanick took an indefinite leave of absence. On June 21, succumbing to pressure from Uber's major investors, Kalanick resigned.

When I heard the news of Travis Kalanick's resignation and read through Eric Holder's report, I felt like a weight had been lifted from my shoulders. I thought back to the struggles of my teenage years, when I had worked so hard to change my future, when I had told myself that I was going to turn my life around, get out of poverty, do something great, be someone great. I thought back to everything that had happened at Penn, from my email to Amy Gutmann to that surreal meeting with the dean of graduate studies. I thought back to my time at Uber, to the jackets, the absurd meetings with HR, the awful things that had happened to me and my friends, and my colleagues who tried to take their own lives. I remembered how afraid I felt when Uber came after me for the blog post; I remembered the private investigators, the rumors, fearing for my own safety, and my meeting with Eric Holder. Throughout my life, I had wanted so badly for everything I'd been through to count for something. And I had wanted so desperately not to be the victim of my story, but the hero.

As I read that report, and saw what happened in the months that followed, I realized that it all had mattered. In some strange way, I felt like I'd been preparing for that moment my entire life. I'd learned from every experience I'd had—from my childhood, from ASU, from Penn, from Plaid, from PubNub, from Uber— and when the time came, when I had an opportunity to stand up against injustice, I was ready to blow the whistle, I was ready to speak up. I'd taken all the bad things that had happened to me, and I'd turned them into something good.

For the first time in many years, I felt like I was truly the sub-ject, not the object, of my own life. I was free.

The day after the news broke that Travis Kalanick had resigned, I took a Lyft home from the city. We crossed the bay and drove across the bridge, and as we passed the exit to Treasure Island, the news on the radio turned to Kalanick's resignation. The driver was listening intently, nodding as the announcer described what had happened. When it went to a commercial break, she turned the volume down and looked right at me in the rearview mirror.

"Can you *believe* it?" she asked, her eyes wide, a look of shock on her face. "With the sexual harassment, and the rape, and now this? That's why I will never drive for Uber. They couldn't even treat their fancy 'real employees' right; why would they treat the drivers any different?" She shook her head. "Can you *believe it*?"

I laughed. "Yeah," I said, "it's pretty crazy."

EPILOGUE

It's difficult for me to believe that by the time this book is published, three years will have passed since I wrote the blog post about my experiences at Uber. So much has happened in that time, and we now live in a very different world. My story about sexual harassment helped spark a movement. In the months that followed, scores of brave women and men stood up and courageously shared their stories of discrimination, sexual harassment, and sexual assault. Their stories changed the world.

After the Holder report and thanks to pressure from the media and public, Uber was finally forced to change. Roxana del Toro and other current and former employees brought a class-action discrimination lawsuit against Uber, which was settled for ten million dollars. In the spring of 2018, faced with employee unrest and in response to an op-ed I wrote for *The New York Times* arguing that ending forced arbitration would do more than anything else to bring an end to workplace discrimination, sexual harassment, and retaliation, Uber finally ended forced arbitration for cases of sexual harassment and sexual assault. And when I asked Dara Khosrowshahi, Uber's new CEO, if Uber still had private investigators following me, he told me that he "killed all that crap." Uber's use of private investigators, he said, was "just insane." It was "unreal what was going on."

My own life has changed quite a bit since the Holder report was released. In the months that followed, I did some advocacy work in the hopes of helping to end the practice of forced arbitration. I worked with federal and state legislators on bills to prohibit it, and, with the help of my lawyer Chris Baker, I filed an amicus curiae brief in the Supreme Court case *Epic Systems Corp. v. Lewis*, asking the court to take my experience at Uber into account when making their decision about arbitration and class-action lawsuits.

In the years that followed, I tried my best to stay out of the news. I'd learned very quickly after the blog post that I was too shy and too introverted to be a public figure; I found all of the media attention overwhelming. The only real interviews I did the year after the blog post were in October 2017, when I spoke to Maureen Dowd of *The New York Times*, and then in December 2017, when *The Financial Times* named me their Person of the Year and *Time* magazine included me as one of the "Silence Breakers" in their Person of the Year issue. It was an incredible honor to be on the cover of *Time*; I'll never forget how humbled I felt sitting for the cover photoshoot, eight months pregnant, next to some of the other incredibly strong women who had bravely spoken up about their mistreatment that year.

I stayed at Stripe until the end of August 2018, working on *Increment* and preparing for the next step in my writing and editing career. I loved the work we were doing, but I wanted to work on something that could influence the world beyond Silicon Valley. I'd seen the global impact that my blog post had, and I wanted to help others share their stories, perspectives, and dreams for the world. In a wonderful coincidence, right after I started looking for a new job, Maureen Dowd told me that *The New York Times* was hiring a technology editor for their opinion section; a few months later, I joined the company.

I feel incredibly blessed to be living my childhood dream, working every day as a writer and editor. My days are filled with editing opinion pieces at *The New York Times*, writing my own books, learning and studying foreign languages and philosophy and mathematics and economics, playing the violin, caring for my sweet daughter (who, as I write this, is waiting for me to put my computer away and read her favorite book, *Go, Dog. Go!*), and spending time with my husband, family, and friends. I wouldn't change it for the world.

I'm living a wonderful new chapter of my life, and I can't wait to see what happens next.

ACKNOWLEDGMENTS

I would like to thank: Bill Weinstein, Sara Nestor, and everyone at Verve, for believing in me; Liz Parker, my amazing literary agent, for keeping me sane and supporting and encouraging all of my wildest writing dreams; Lindsey Schwoeri, Lindsay Prevette, Rebecca Marsh, Linda Friedner, and everyone at Viking who brought this book to life; my brilliant publicist Rebecca Taylor; my friends and coworkers from Uber, especially Roxana del Toro, Eamon Bisson-Donahue, and Rick Boone; Maureen Dowd, James Bennet, Jim Dao, Katie Kingsbury, Clay Risen, and all of my colleagues at *The New York Times*; the many wonderful people who have believed in me, supported me, and inspired me, especially Sarah Lacy, Paul Carr, Greg Bensinger, Chris Baker, Deborah Schwartz, Kristin Burr, Margit Wennmachers, Claire Schmidt, Charles Yao, Gretchen Carlson, and Ashley Judd; all of my friends who have endlessly supported and loved me over the years; my family, especially Martha, Sara, and Peter; Shalon van Tine, who has been the greatest, kindest, closest friend ever since the day we met; my beautiful, sweet daughter; and, above all, my husband Chad—there's no one I'd rather walk through life with. To all of you, I owe this book.

APPENDIX A:
RESOURCES

If you are experiencing mistreatment in the workplace, you can find a lawyer through the National Employment Lawyers Association (www.nela.org) or your local bar association.

If you are a victim of discrimination, harassment, or retaliation in the workplace, you can file a complaint with the Equal Employment Opportunity Commission (the government agency that enforces civil rights laws). Complaints must be filed within 180 days of the incident, and you do not need a lawyer to file a complaint. File online here: www.eeoc.gov.

If you are the victim of sexual violence, harassment, or discrimination at school, you can file a complaint with the U.S. Department of Education's Office for Civil Rights: www2.ed.gov /about/offices/list/ocr/docs/howto.html.

If you are the victim of sexual assault, you can contact RAINN (www.rainn.org) for support and advice. If you are the victim of sexual harassment, you can find help through Better Brave (www .betterbrave.org/where-to-find-help).

Reflecting on One Very, Very Strange Year at Uber

February 19, 2017

As most of you know, I left Uber in December and joined Stripe in January. I've gotten a lot of questions over the past couple of months about why I left and what my time at Uber was like. It's a strange, fascinating, and slightly horrifying story that deserves to be told while it is still fresh in my mind, so here we go.

I joined Uber as a site reliability engineer (SRE) back in November 2015, and it was a great time to join as an engineer. They were still wrangling microservices out of their monolithic API, and things were just chaotic enough that there was exciting reliability work to be done. The SRE team was still pretty new when

I joined, and I had the rare opportunity to choose whichever team was working on something that I wanted to be part of.

After the first couple of weeks of training, I chose to join the team that worked on my area of expertise, and this is where things started getting weird. On my first official day rotating on the team, my new manager sent me a string of messages over company chat. He was in an open relationship, he said, and his girlfriend was having an easy time finding new partners but he wasn't. He was trying to stay out of trouble at work, he said, but he couldn't help getting in trouble, because he was looking for women to have sex with. It was clear that he was trying to get me to have sex with him, and it was so clearly out of line that I immediately took screenshots of these chat messages and reported him to HR.

Uber was a pretty good-sized company at that time, and I had pretty standard expectations of how they would handle situations like this. I expected that I would report him to HR, they would handle the situation appropriately, and then life would go on— unfortunately, things played out quite a bit differently. When I reported the situation, I was told by both HR and upper management that even though this was clearly sexual harassment and he was propositioning me, it was this man's first offense, and that they wouldn't feel comfortable giving him anything other than a warning and a stern talking-to. Upper management told me that he "was a high performer" (i.e., had stellar performance reviews from his superiors) and they wouldn't feel comfortable punishing him for what was probably just an innocent mistake on his part.

I was then told that I had to make a choice: (1) I could either go and find another team and then never have to interact with this man again, or (2) I could stay on the team, but I would have to understand that he would most likely give me a poor performance review when review time came around, and there was nothing they could do about that. I remarked that this didn't seem like much of a choice and that I wanted to stay on the team because I had significant expertise in the exact project that the team was struggling to complete (it was genuinely in the company's best interest to have me on that team), but they told me the same thing again and again. One HR rep even explicitly told me that it wouldn't be retaliation if I received a negative review later because I had been "given an option." I tried to escalate the situation but got nowhere with either HR or my own management chain (who continued to insist that they had given him a stern talking-to and didn't want to ruin his career over his "first offense").

So I left that team, and took quite a few weeks learning about other teams before landing anywhere (I desperately wanted to not have to interact with HR ever again). I ended up joining a brand-new SRE team that gave me a lot of autonomy, and I found ways to be happy and do amazing work. In fact, the work I did on this team turned into the production-readiness process which I wrote about in my bestselling (!!!) book *Production-Ready Microservices*.

Over the next few months, I began to meet more women engineers in the company. As I got to know them and heard their stories, I was surprised that some of them had stories similar to my own. Some of the women even had stories about reporting the exact same manager I had reported, and had reported inappropriate interactions with him long before I had even joined the company. It became obvious that both HR and management had been lying about this being "his first offense," and it certainly wasn't his last. Within a few months, he was reported once again for inappropriate behavior, and those who reported him were told it was still his "first offense." The situation was escalated as far up the chain as it could be escalated, and still nothing was done.

Myself and a few of the women who had reported him in the past decided to all schedule meetings with HR to insist that something be done. In my meeting, the rep I spoke with told me that he had never been reported before, he had only ever committed one offense (in his chats with me), and that none of the other women who they met with had anything bad to say about him, so no further action could or would be taken. It was such a blatant lie that there was really nothing I could do. There was nothing any of us could do. We all gave up on Uber HR and our managers after that. Eventually he "left" the company. I don't know what he did that finally convinced them to fire him.

In the background, there was a game-of-thrones political war raging within the ranks of upper management in the infrastructure engineering organization. It seemed like every manager was fighting their peers and attempting to undermine their direct supervisor so that they could have their direct supervisor's job. No attempts were made by these managers to hide what they were doing: they boasted about it in meetings, told their direct reports about it, and the like. I remember countless meetings with my managers and skip-levels where I would sit there, not saying anything, and the manager would be boasting about finding favor with their skip-level and that I should expect them to have their manager's job within a quarter or two. I also remember a very disturbing team meeting in which one of the directors boasted to our team that he had withheld business-critical information from one of the executives so that he could curry favor with one of the other executives (and, he told us with a smile on his face, it worked!).

The ramifications of these political games were significant: projects were abandoned left and right, OKRs were changed multiple times each quarter, nobody knew what our organizational priorities would be one day to the next, and very little ever got done. We all lived under fear that our teams would be dissolved, there would be another re-org, and we'd have to start on yet another new project with an impossible deadline. It was an organization in complete, unrelenting chaos.

I was lucky enough during all of this to work with some of the most amazing engineers in the Bay Area. We kept our heads down and did good (sometimes great) work despite the chaos. We loved our work, we loved the engineering challenges, we loved making this crazy Uber machine work, and together we found ways to make it through the re-orgs and the changing OKRs and the abandoned projects and the impossible deadlines. We kept each other sane, kept the gigantic Uber ecosystem running, and told ourselves that it would eventually get better.

Things didn't get better, and engineers began transferring to the less chaotic engineering organizations. Once I had finished up my projects and saw that things weren't going to change, I also requested a transfer. I met all of the qualifications for transferring—I had managers who wanted me on their teams, and I had a perfect performance score—so I didn't see how anything could go wrong. And then my transfer was blocked.

According to my manager, his manager, and the director, my transfer was being blocked because I had undocumented performance problems. I pointed out that I had a perfect performance score, and that there had never been any complaints about my performance. I had completed all OKRs on schedule, never missed a deadline even in the insane organizational chaos, and that I had managers waiting for me to join their team. I asked what my performance problem was, and they didn't give me an answer. At first they said I wasn't being technical enough, so I pointed out that they were the ones who had given me my OKRs, and if they wanted to see different work from me, then they should give me the kind of work they wanted to see—they then backed down and stopped saying that this was the problem. I kept pushing, until finally I was told that "performance problems aren't always something that has to do with work, but sometimes can be about things outside of work or your personal life." I couldn't decipher that, so I gave up and decided to stay until my next performance review.

Performance review season came around, and I received a great review with no complaints whatsoever about my performance. I waited a couple of months, and then attempted to transfer again. When I attempted to transfer, I was told that my performance review and score had been changed after the official reviews had been calibrated, and so I was no longer eligible for transfer. When I asked management why my review had been changed after the fact (and why hadn't they let me know that they'd changed it?), they said that I didn't show any signs of an upward career trajectory. I pointed out that I was publishing a book with O'Reilly, speaking at major tech conferences, and doing all of the things that you're supposed to do to have an "upward career trajectory," but they said it didn't matter and I needed to prove myself as an engineer. I was stuck where I was.

I asked them to change my performance review back. My manager said that the new negative review I was given had no real-world consequences, so I shouldn't worry about it. But I went home and cried that day, because even aside from impacts to my salary and bonuses, it did have real-world consequences— significant consequences that my management chain was very well aware of. I was enrolled in a Stanford CS graduate program, sponsored by Uber, and Uber only sponsored employees who had high performance scores. Under both of my official performance reviews and scores, I qualified for the program, but after this sneaky new negative score I was no longer eligible.

It turned out that keeping me on the team made my manager look good, and I overheard him boasting to the rest of the team that even though the rest of the teams were losing their women engineers left and right, he still had some on his team.

When I joined Uber, the organization I was part of was over 25% women. By the time I was trying to transfer to another eng organization, this number had dropped down to less than 6%. Women were transferring out of the organization, and those who couldn't transfer were quitting or preparing to quit. There were two major reasons for this: there was the organizational chaos, and there was also the sexism within the organization. When I asked our director at an org all-hands about what was being done about the dwindling numbers of women in the org compared to the rest of the company, his reply was, in a nutshell, that the women of Uber just needed to step up and be better engineers.

Things were beginning to get even more comically absurd with each passing day. Every time something ridiculous happened, every time a sexist email was sent, I'd sent a short report to HR just to keep a record going. Things came to a head with one particular email chain from the director of our engineering organization concerning leather jackets that had been ordered for all of the SREs. See, earlier in the year, the organization had promised leather jackets for everyone in organization, and had taken all of our sizes; we all tried them on and found our sizes, and placed our orders. One day, all of the women (there were, I believe, six of us left in the org) received an email saying that no leather jackets were being ordered for the women because there were not enough women in the organization to justify placing an order. I replied and said that I was sure Uber SRE could find room in their budget to buy leather jackets for the, what, *six women* if it could afford to buy them for *over a hundred and twenty men*. The director replied back, saying that if we women really wanted equality, then we should realize we were getting equality by not getting the leather jackets. He said that because there were so many men in the org, they had gotten a significant discount on the men's jackets but not on the women's jackets, and it wouldn't be equal or fair, he argued, to give the women leather jackets that cost a little more than the men's jackets. We were told that if we wanted leather jackets, we women needed to find jackets that were the same price as the bulk-order price of the men's jackets.

I forwarded this absurd chain of emails to HR, and they requested to meet with me shortly after. I don't know what I expected after all of my earlier encounters with them, but this one
was more ridiculous than I could have ever imagined. The HR rep
began the meeting by asking me if I had noticed that *I* was the
common theme in all of the reports I had been making, and that
if I had ever considered that I might be the problem. I pointed out
that everything I had reported came with extensive documentation and I clearly wasn't the instigator (or even a main character)
in the majority of them—she countered by saying that there was
absolutely no record in HR of any of the incidents I was claiming
I had reported (which, of course, was a lie, and I reminded her I
had email and chat records to prove it was a lie). She then asked
me if women engineers at Uber were friends and talked a lot, and
then asked me how often we communicated, what we talked
about, what email addresses we used to communicate, which chat
rooms we frequented, etc.—an absurd and insulting request that I
refused to comply with. When I pointed out how few women were
in SRE, she recounted a story about how sometimes certain people of certain genders and ethnic backgrounds were better suited
for some jobs than others, so I shouldn't be surprised by the gender ratios in engineering. Our meeting ended with her berating
me about keeping email records of things, and told me it was unprofessional to report things via email to HR.

Less than a week after this absurd meeting, my manager scheduled a 1:1 with me and told me we needed to have a difficult conversation. He told me I was on very thin ice for reporting his
manager to HR. California is an at-will employment state, he said,

which means we can fire you if you ever do this again. I told him that was illegal, and he replied that he had been a manager for a long time, he knew what was illegal, and threatening to fire me for reporting things to HR was not illegal. I reported his threat immediately after the meeting to both HR and to the CTO: they both admitted that this was illegal, but none of them did anything. (I was told much later that they didn't do anything because the manager who threatened me "was a high performer.")

I had a new job offer in my hands less than a week later.

On my last day at Uber, I calculated the percentage of women who were still in the org. Out of over 150 engineers in the SRE teams, only 3% were women.

When I look back at the time I spent at Uber, I'm overcome with thankfulness that I had the opportunity to work with some of the best engineers around. I'm proud of the work I did, I'm proud of the impact that I was able to make on the entire organization, and I'm proud that the work I did and wrote a book about has been adopted by other tech companies all over the world. And when I think about the things I've recounted in the paragraphs above, I feel a lot of sadness, but I can't help but laugh at how ridiculous everything was. Such a strange experience. Such a strange year.